# Fun and Easy
# Paper Airplanes

Happy Birthday
6-1-12

To:
Chance
with Love ♡
From:
Jeanne
and Andrew Dewar

# Contents

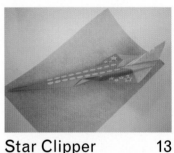

Delta Delta            16

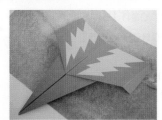

Star Fighter           17

Gold Bug               18

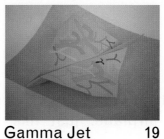

Gamma Jet              19

Spectre                20

Phoenix                21

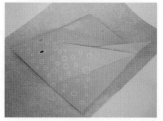

Stingray               22

Javelin                23

## Design Your Own Planes    24

Folding Paper

# Introduction

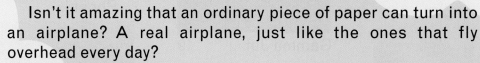

Isn't it amazing that an ordinary piece of paper can turn into an airplane? A real airplane, just like the ones that fly overhead every day?

Those airplanes, full of people flying here and there, have engines to help them take off and fly long distances. Paper airplanes may not have the engines, but if you fold them right and throw them carefully, they will fly just the same.

All airplanes need wings and balance. With origami planes, you get balance by folding your paper so that there are wings at the back, and lots of weight at the front.

This book is filled with directions for folding planes that will really fly, and paper you can use to make them. Even when the paper is gone and your airplanes all flown away, you can use these directions with your own paper to make a whole new fleet of amazing origami airplanes.

# How to Fold

Here's what the arrows in the directions mean:

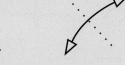

**Fold this way**  **Fold and reopen**  **Fold around behind**  **Flip the whole plane over**

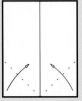 Most planes start with the paper face down. The drawings show the face in dark colors, and the back in lighter colors.

This is a mountain fold; it looks like a bit like a mountain.

And this is a valley fold.

 Rudders are made with reverse folds. Start by creasing the paper along the fold lines. Open out the plane slightly, reverse each of the folds, and recrease them to make a neat rudder.

 Most of the planes need a final tweak to really fly well. They will dive until you bend up the back edge of the wing slightly. Bending the wing keeps the nose up and lets the plane float on the air. But bend it too much, and the plane will stall and crash. Bend the back edge more or less until the plane flies just right.

# How to Fly the Planes

Your plane won't fly well unless it's straight. Hold it at arm's length and check.

If not, carefully twist the wings and tail until they are.

The plane will go from this...

...to this.

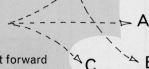

 A

C B

Test fly the plane by tossing it firmly straight forward and watching how it flies. If it stalls or dives, adjust it and test fly again, until it glides gently like pattern A.

**A**

Just right!

**B**

Fix a stall by bending the back of the wing down slightly.

**C**

Fix a dive by bending the back of the wing up slightly.

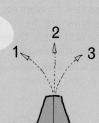

2

1   3

If your plane turns to one side or the other, adjust it until it flies straight as in line 2.

**1**

Fix a left turn by bending up the back edge of the right wing slightly.

**2**

Just right!

**3**

Fix a right turn by bending up the back edge of the left wing slightly.

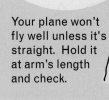

Indoors, all you need is a gentle toss to get a good flight. Push the plane straight ahead, parallel to the floor, at about the same speed as the glide.

On calm, dry days you can take your planes out to the park. Try throwing them straight up, as high as you can. This is how world record flights begin...except that they are made in sports stadiums. Can you beat 28 seconds?

If there is enough room, you can throw a little harder, but still basically straight ahead. Be sure not to hit anyone, break anything, or poke any eyes!

# Diamond Dart

You've probably made lots of paper darts. But I'll bet you've never made one from square paper. There are lots of ways to do it, and I've made a box full of them. I think this one looks and flies best. What do you think?

### 1
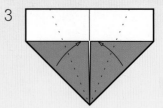

Start with the paper face down, and fold on line 1.

### 2
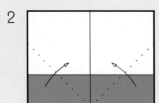

Fold up on the 2 lines.

### 3
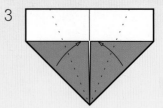

Fold up on the 3 lines.

### 4
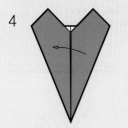

Fold the plane in half towards you.

### 5
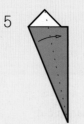

Fold the wings down along the 4 lines.

### 6

Here's how it will look. Bend the wings back out and you're finished!

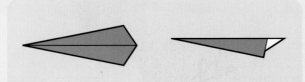

# Wave Rider

One of the fun things about origami is that you can fiddle and fly, fiddle and fly, fiddle and fly again. It doesn't take long to make a new plane, so you can try lots of different ideas. Even if a new plane doesn't look like it should fly, give it a try! Wave Rider is a good example of what might happen.

1

Start with the paper face down, fold on the 1 lines, and open it out again.

2

Fold on the 2 lines.

3

Fold on the 3 lines.

4

Refold on the 1 lines.

5

Fold the plane in half away from you.

6

Fold the wings down on the 4 lines.

7

Fold the fins down on the 5 lines. Open the plane out like the photo and you're done!

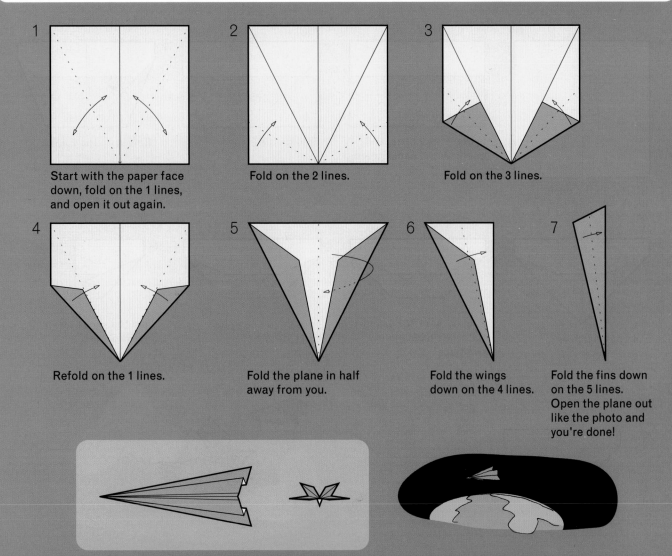

# Soarer

Lots of weight in the nose makes this plane a stable and steady flier. You can throw it very hard outside, but keep your eye on it. It might go farther than you expect!

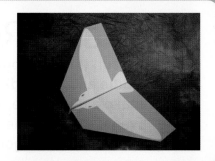

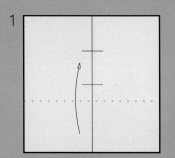

**1**

Start with the paper face down, and fold on line 1.

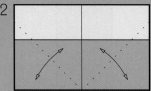

**2**

Fold on the 2 lines, and open out the paper again.

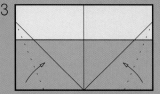

**3**

Fold on the 3 lines.

**4**

Refold on the 2 lines.

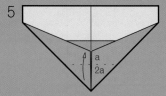

**5**

Fold up on line 4.

**6**

Fold back on line 5, and tuck the tip behind the two flaps.

**7**

Fold the plane in half away from you.

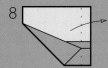

**8**

Fold the wings down on the 6 lines.

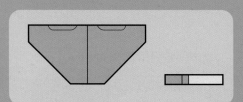

# Cloud

Here is another dart. This one has lots of weight in the nose for stability, but also big wings for long flights.

1
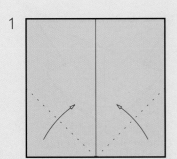
Start with the paper face down, and fold on the 1 lines.

2
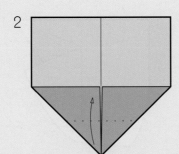
Fold up the tip on line 2.

3
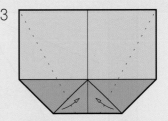
Fold up on the 3 lines.

4
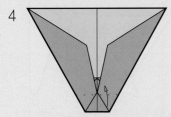
Fold up on line 4.

5
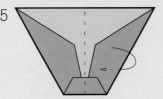
Fold the plane in half away from you.

6
2a | a
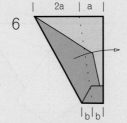

b | b
Fold the wings down on the 5 lines.

7

Open the wings out again and you're done!

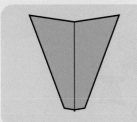

11

# Jumping Jack

Jumping Jack is a new version of the classic Japanese "squid plane." The first few folds look hard, but I think you'll find them easier than you thought. Once you're done folding, try flying it outdoors. This plane needs lots of room!

1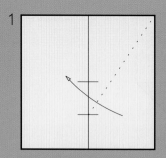

Start with the paper face down, and fold on the right line 1.

2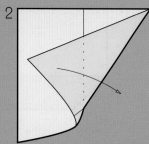

Fold the paper back on the right line 2.

3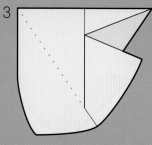

Make the same folds on the left side.

4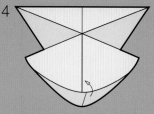

Crease the paper along the 3 lines.

5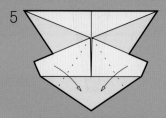

Fold down on the 4 lines.

6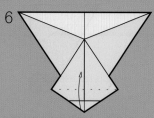

Fold the tip up on line 5.

7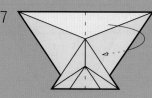

Fold the plane in half away from you.

8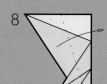

Fold the wings down on the 6 lines.

9

Open the wings out again and you're done!

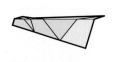

# Star Clipper

One day there may be starliners that can take off and land at airports, and fly through space on their way around the world. And when there are, they may look like this. Star Clipper looks very high-tech, but it's really easy to fold.

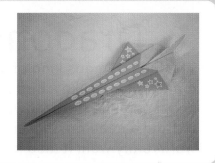

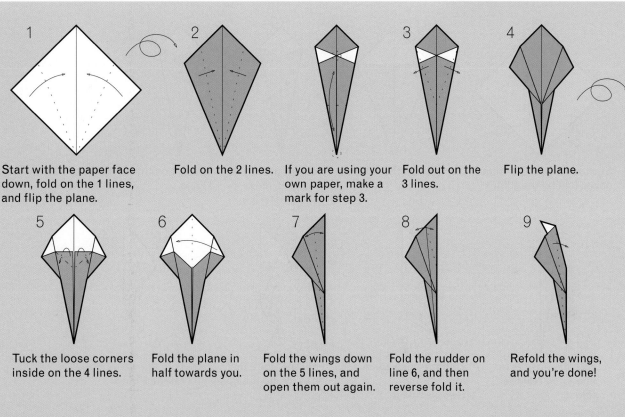

**1** Start with the paper face down, fold on the 1 lines, and flip the plane.

**2** Fold on the 2 lines. If you are using your own paper, make a mark for step 3.

**3** Fold out on the 3 lines.

**4** Flip the plane.

**5** Tuck the loose corners inside on the 4 lines.

**6** Fold the plane in half towards you.

**7** Fold the wings down on the 5 lines, and open them out again.

**8** Fold the rudder on line 6, and then reverse fold it.

**9** Refold the wings, and you're done!

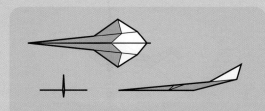

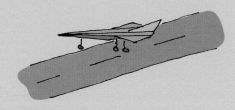

# Dragon Boat

The most famous kind of Japanese origami is the folded crane. It looks like a bird in flight, but the balance is wrong and it can't be flown. I wanted to make a flying bird, and putting a head on a version of the Star Clipper turned out to work really well. It also looks a bit like a viking ship.

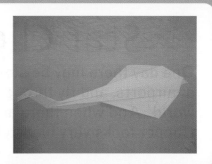

**1**

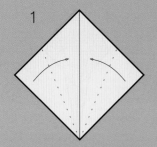

Start with the paper face down, fold on the 1 lines.

**2**

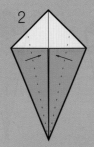

Fold on the 2 lines.

If you are using your own paper, make a mark for step 3.

**3**

Fold out on the 3 lines.

**4**

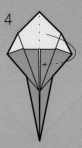

Fold the plane in half away from you.

**5**

Fold the nose at line 4 and reverse fold it.

**6**

Fold the nose again at line 5 and reverse fold it.

**7**

Fold the tip of the nose inside the head.

**8**

Fold the wings down on the 6 lines.

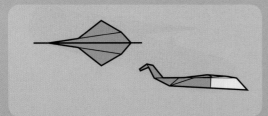

# Alpha Jet

This is a very simple plane, but it looks and flies just like a fighter jet. The small, delta-shaped wings make it very slick and speedy. How will it fly outdoors? High and far? Or straight and fast?

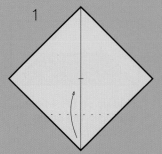

**1**

Start with the paper face down, and fold on line 1.

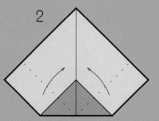

**2**

Fold up on the 2 lines.

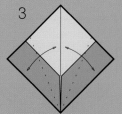

**3**

Fold up on the 3 lines, and open the paper out again.

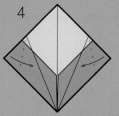

**4**

Fold down on the 4 lines.

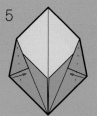

**5**

Fold down on the 5 lines.

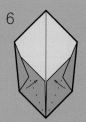

**6**

Refold the 3 lines.

**7**

Fold the plane in half away from you.

**8**

Fold the wings down on the 6 lines, and open them out again.

**9**

Fold the rudder on line 7, and then reverse fold it.

**10**

Fold the wings down again, and you're done!

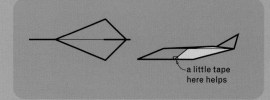

a little tape here helps

# Delta Delta

Triangular wings are called delta wings, because they look like the Greek letter delta (Δ). Many paper airplanes are delta wing planes. This plane has triangular rudders on the ends of its triangular wings: a delta delta plane.

**1**
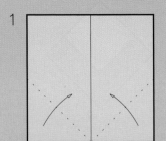
Start with the paper face down, and fold on the 1 lines.

**2**
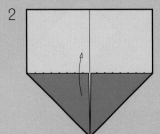
Fold up on line 2.

**3**
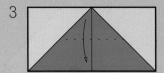
Fold down on line 3.

**4**
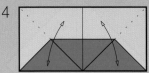
Fold up on the 4 lines, and open the paper out again.

**5**
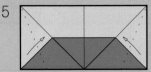
Fold up on the 5 lines.

**6**

Refold on the 4 lines, and fold the plane in half away from you.

**7**
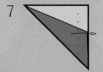
Fold the wings down on the 6 lines.

**8**

Fold the wingtips up on the 7 lines. Open out the wings and you're done!

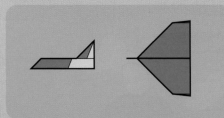

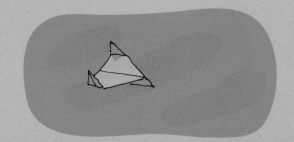

# Star Fighter

This plane looked to me like the kind of plane you might see in a science fiction movie. That's why it's called Star Fighter. Planes with wings this far back won't fly straight without rudders on the wingtips. Turning them down seems to work better than turning them up. Looking futuristic is a bonus!

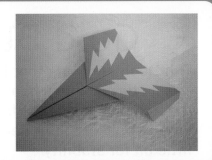

**1**

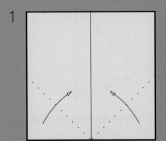

Start with the paper face down, and fold on the 1 lines.

**2**

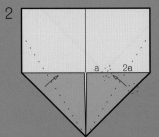

Fold up on the 2 lines. If you are using your own paper, fold as shown.

**3**

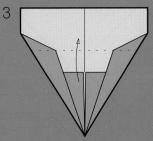

Fold up on line 3.

**4**

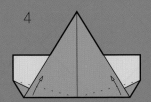

Fold up on the 4 lines.

**5**

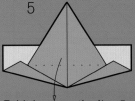

Fold down on the line 5.

**6**

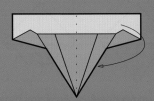

Fold the plane in half away from you.

**7**

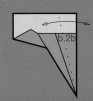

Fold the wings down on the 6 lines as shown. Open them out again.

**8**

Fold the wingtips down on the 7 lines, and refold the wings.

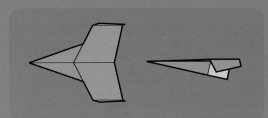

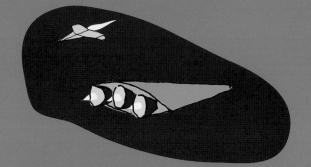

17

# Gold Bug

A little fiddling, another fold or two, and an ordinary sort of design turned into a beetle! The Gold Bug is a little thick at the front and may be stiff, but the finished plane will look great. You'll probably need to turn up the back of the wing a little bit for stability.

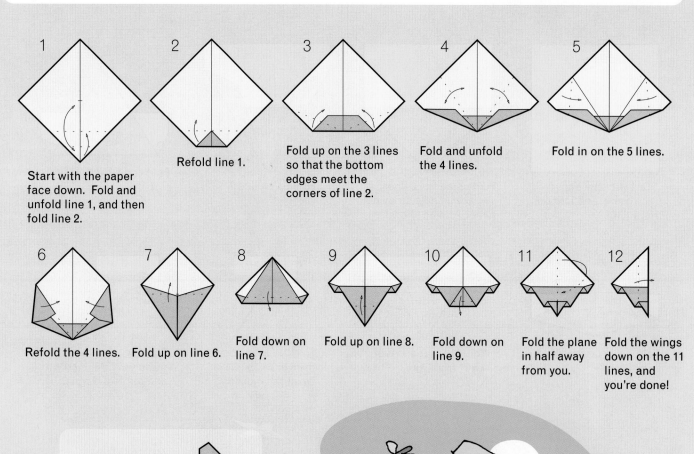

**1** Start with the paper face down. Fold and unfold line 1, and then fold line 2.

**2** Refold line 1.

**3** Fold up on the 3 lines so that the bottom edges meet the corners of line 2.

**4** Fold and unfold the 4 lines.

**5** Fold in on the 5 lines.

**6** Refold the 4 lines.

**7** Fold up on line 6.

**8** Fold down on line 7.

**9** Fold up on line 8.

**10** Fold down on line 9.

**11** Fold the plane in half away from you.

**12** Fold the wings down on the 11 lines, and you're done!

# Gamma Jet

This is a very exotic version of the classic Japanese "belly button" plane. The belly button is the triangual tab at the bottom that holds everything together. The classic is a simple dart, but the Gamma Jet has become a next-generation stealth fighter!

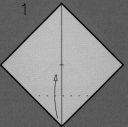

**1**

Start with the paper face down, and fold on line 1.

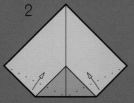

**2**

Fold up on the 2 lines.

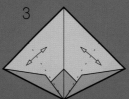

**3**

Fold and unfold the 3 lines.

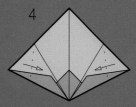

**4**

Fold down on the 4 lines.

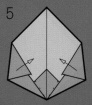

**5**

Refold on the 3 lines.

**6**

Fold up on line 5.

**7**

Fold up on the 6 lines, so the edges are parallel.

**8**

Fold down on line 7.

**9**

Fold the plane in half away from you.

**10**

Fold the wings down on the 8 lines.

**11**

Fold, unfold, and reverse fold the rudder on line 9.

**12**

Refold the wings, and you're done.

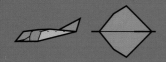

# Spectre

Most origami airplanes have their wings at the back, with maybe a little extra wing at the front. But most real airplanes have a tail at the back. After a lot of trying, I was finally able to fold one with a proper tail, and it looks a bit like a bird. Or maybe it's an angel, or a ghost?

1

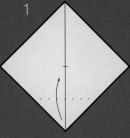

Start with the paper face down, and fold on line 1.

2

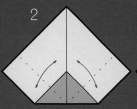

Fold up on the 2 lines, and open out the paper again.

3

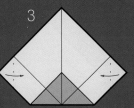

Fold in on the 3 lines.

4

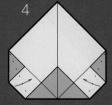

Fold up on the 4 lines.

5

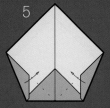

Refold the 2 lines.

6

Fold the sides behind the plane on the 5 lines.

7

Fold the top layer only on the 6 lines to bring the sides back out from behind.

8

Fold up on line 7.

9

Fold down on line 8.

10

Fold the plane in half away from you.

11

Fold the wings down on the 9 lines, and you're done!

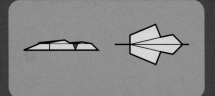

# Phoenix

The phoenix is an immortal, mythical bird that ends its life in flames and is reborn from the ashes. I don't know what a phoenix looks like because I've never seen one, but it might just be like this!

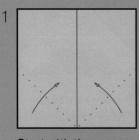

1

Start with the paper face down, and fold on the 1 lines.

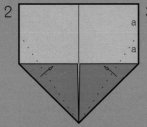

2

Fold up on the 2 lines, starting half-way up the sides.

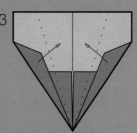

3

Fold up on the 3 lines.

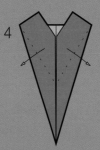

4

Fold down on the 4 lines.

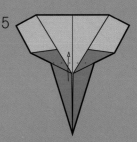

5

Fold the nose up on line 5.

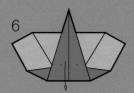

6

Fold the nose down again on line 6.

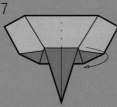

7

Fold the plane in half away from you.

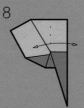

8

Fold and unfold the wings on the 7 lines.

9

Fold and reverse fold the neck at line 8.

10

Fold and reverse fold the head at line 9.

11

Fold the wings down again, and you're done!

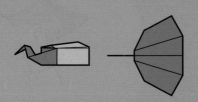

# Stingray

This kind of three-dimensional plane looks difficult, but it really isn't any different from other planes. The trickiest parts are the double reverse fold, and taping the plane together without getting it twisted. But I think you'll find it well worth the tiny extra effort.

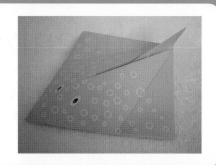

**1**

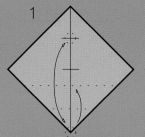

Start with the paper face down. Fold and reopen on line 1. Fold up on line 2.

**2**

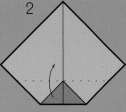

Fold up line 1 again.

**3**

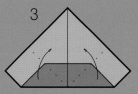

Fold up on the 3 lines.

**4**

a a

If you're using your own paper, make marks where shown. Reopen the paper.

**5**

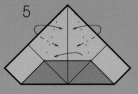

Fold backwards on the 4 lines, reopen the paper, and fold the plane in half toward you.

**6**

Fold up on line 5.

**7**

Fold down on line 6.

**8**

Reverse the two rudder folds, and then open out the plane again.

**9**

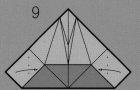

Fold in on the 7 lines.

**10**

Fold up on the 8 lines.

**11**

Fold up on the 3 lines again.

**12**

Push the sides of the rudder together and refold all of the fold lines.

**13**

tape

Use bits of tape to hold the rudder and the front flaps together as shown.

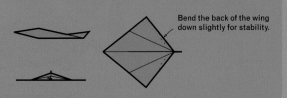

Bend the back of the wing down slightly for stability.

# Javelin

This plane looks a little like a British jet fighter called the Javelin. There are more steps than usual, and it may take a little time to fold, but it is well worth it. Practice the double reverse folds for the wings and rudder once or twice before using the paper from this book.

**1**

Start with the paper face down, and fold on lines 1 and 2.

**2**

Refold on line 1.

**3**

Fold up on the 3 lines.

**4**

Starting at the thick spot at the marks, fold up on the 4 lines.

**5**

Fold down on the 5 lines.

**6**

before    after

Reverse fold both wings.

**7**

Fold the loose edges inwards on the 6 lines.

**8**

Fold the corners inwards on the 7 lines.

**9**

Fold the plane in half towards you.

**10**

Fold the rudder on line 8.

**11**

Fold the rudder again on line 9.

**12**

Reverse fold the rudder.

**13**

2b   3b

Fold and unfold at line 10.

**14**

Fold and unfold at line 11.

**15**

Fold up the wings, and then open out the whole plane.

**16**

Fold the corners inwards on the 12 lines.

**17**

Refold all the folds and pull the plane together.

**18**

tape

tape

Tape the nose, the back of the rudder, and the tail.

Bend the back of the stabilizer up slightly for stability.

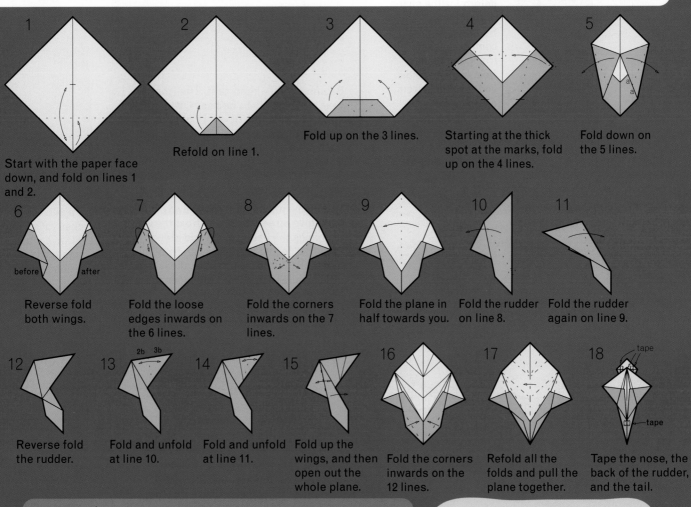

# Design Your Own Planes

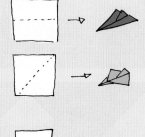

The kind of paper you use, and the direction of the center fold, will determine the shape of your plane. Square paper makes compact planes: triangular planes from straight folds, and diamonds from diagonal folds. Rectangular paper lets you make short and wide, or long and pointy planes.

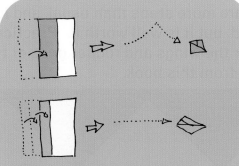

Balance is very important. The front of your plane needs to be heavy, which means folding lots of layers of paper. If your plane stalls, make extra folds at the front to improve the balance.

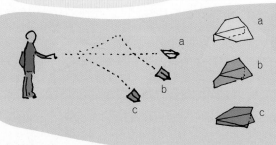

Your plane might not fly right away, but don't give up yet! You can refold the wings to change the balance and add stability. Plane "a" is just right. You can fix planes that stall (like "b") by making the wings a little smaller at the front or bigger at the back. Planes that dive (like "c") can be fixed by making the back part of the fuselage bigger and changing the balance.

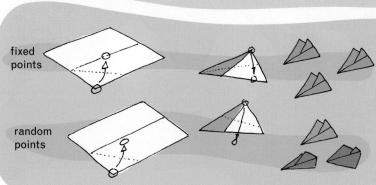

fixed points

random points

Once your plane starts really flying, you'll want to make more. But if you've just folded randomly, your next plane won't be quite the same. Always fold to fixed points—edge to edge, corner to corner, corner to edge, or at half-way points—and every plane will turn out just right.

If your planes still don't fly, just wad them up and toss them... You can always start again with a fresh sheet of paper.

DIAMOND DRAFT

4  4

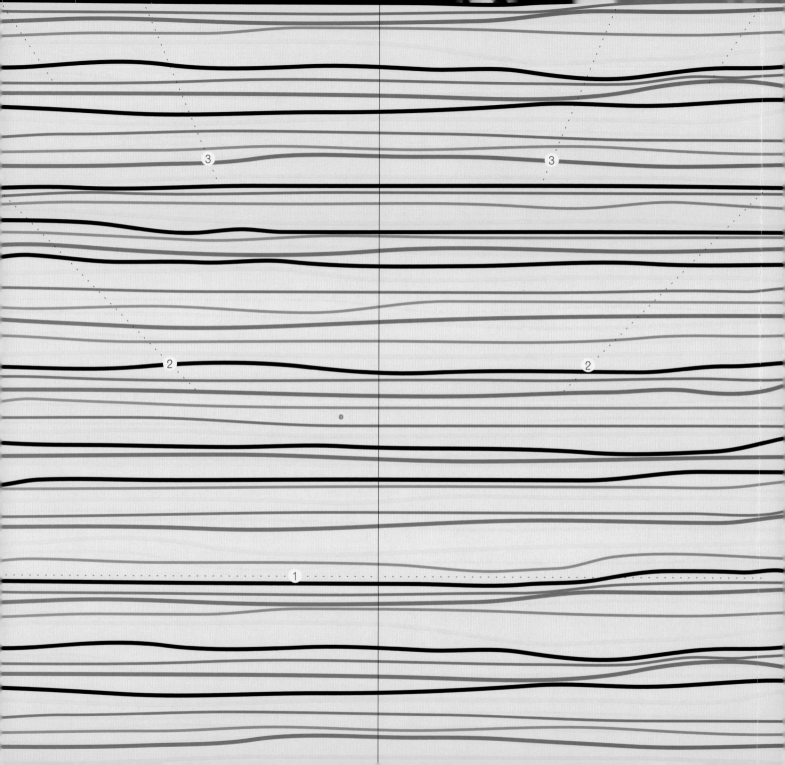

4  4

DIAMOND DART

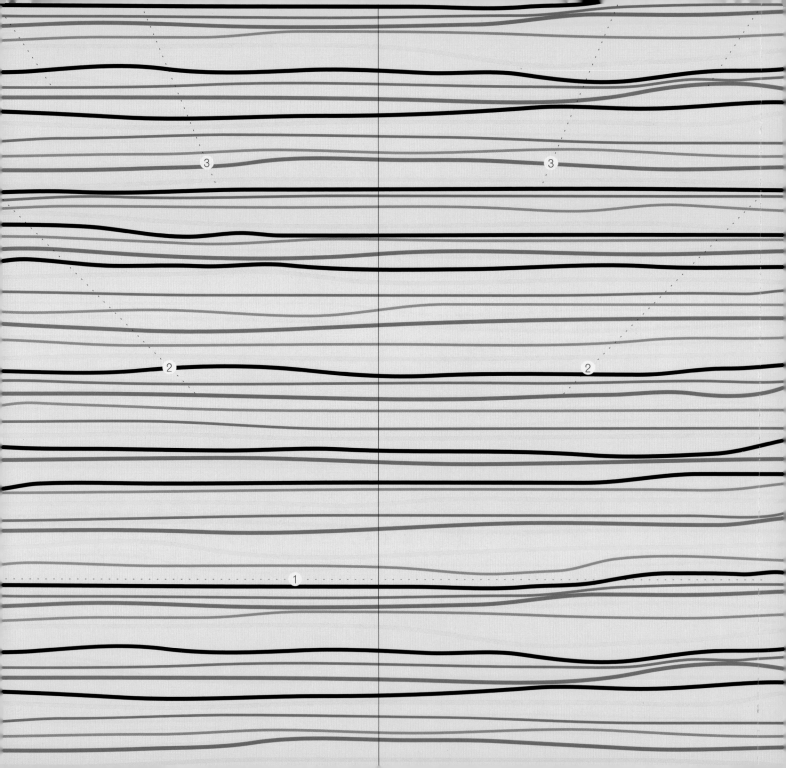

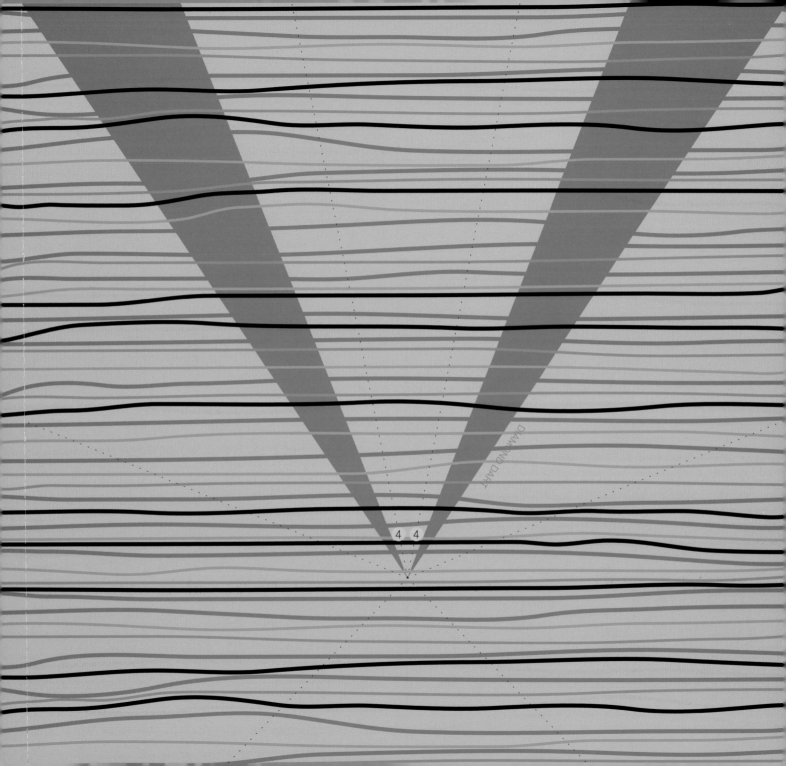

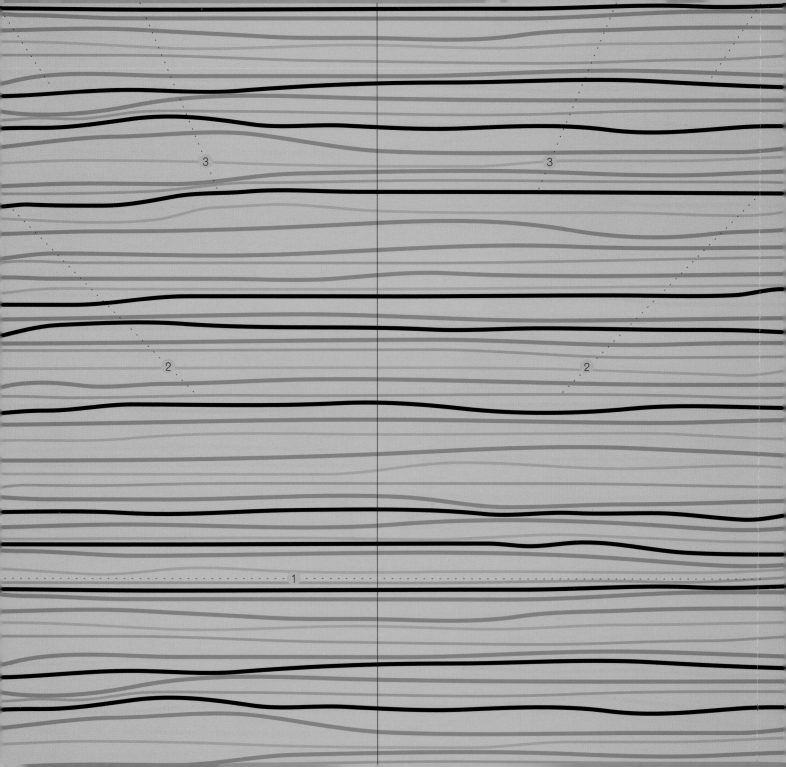

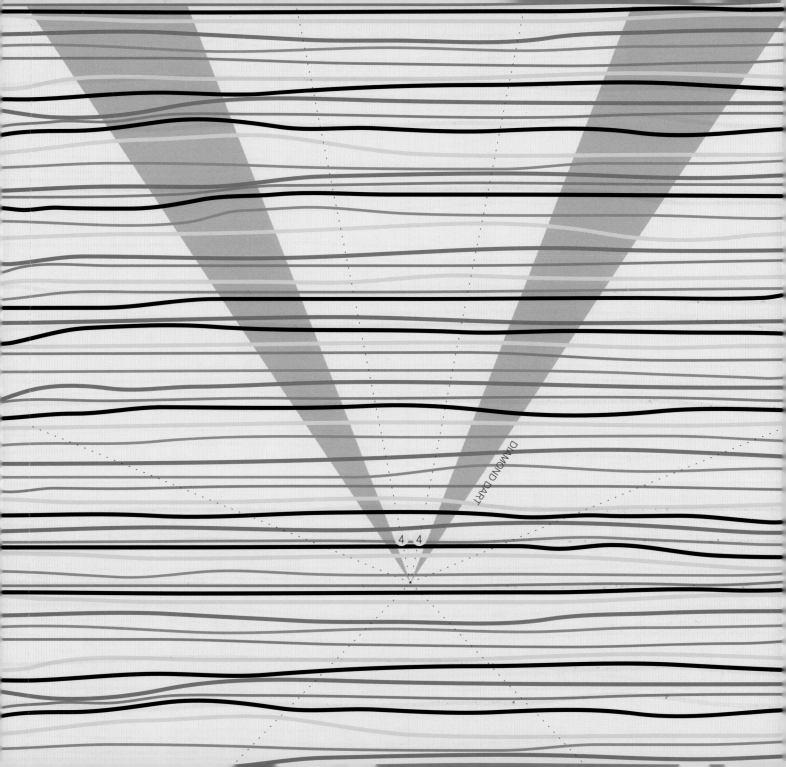

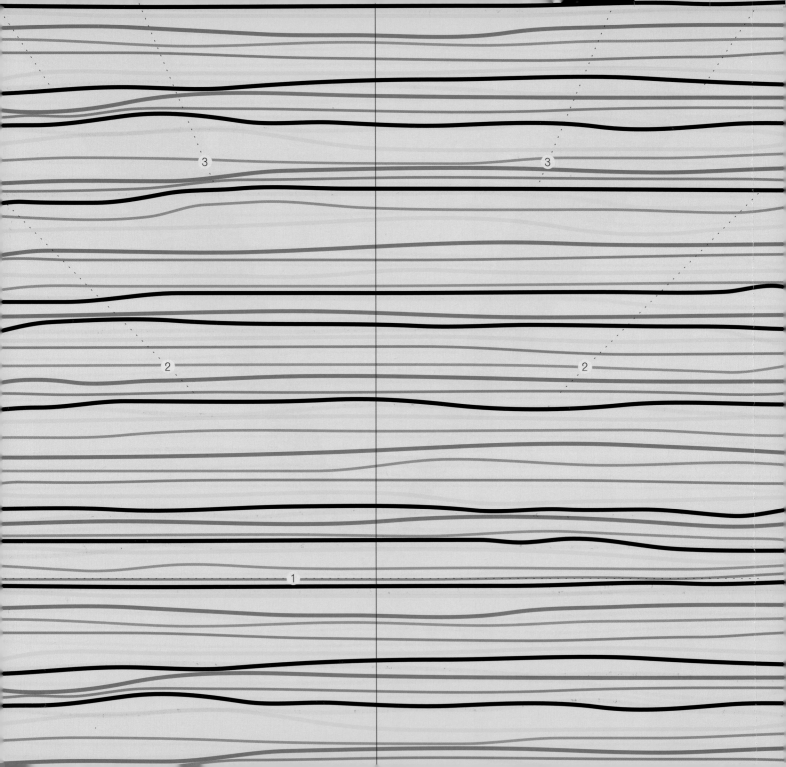

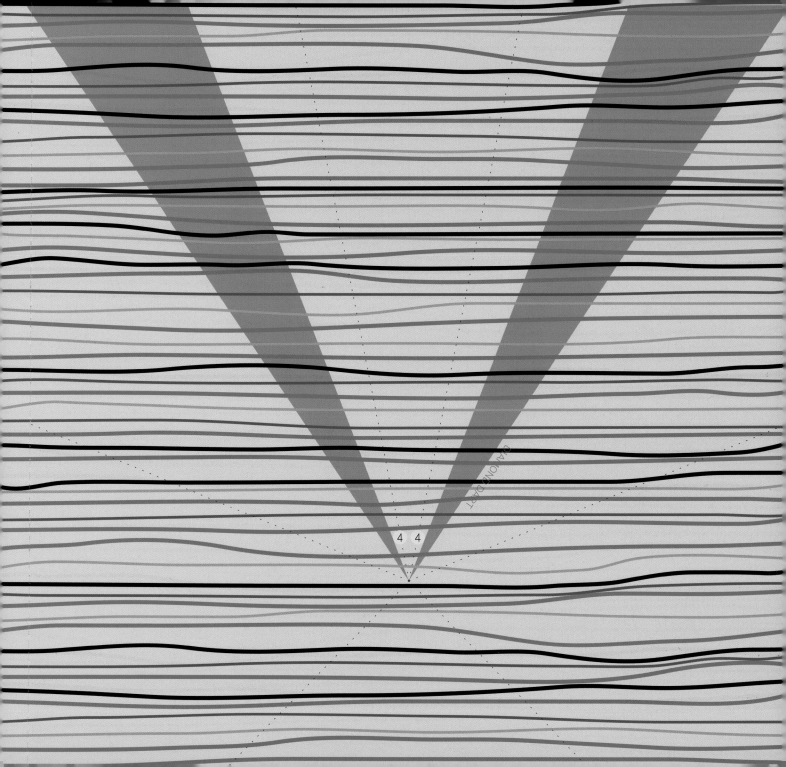

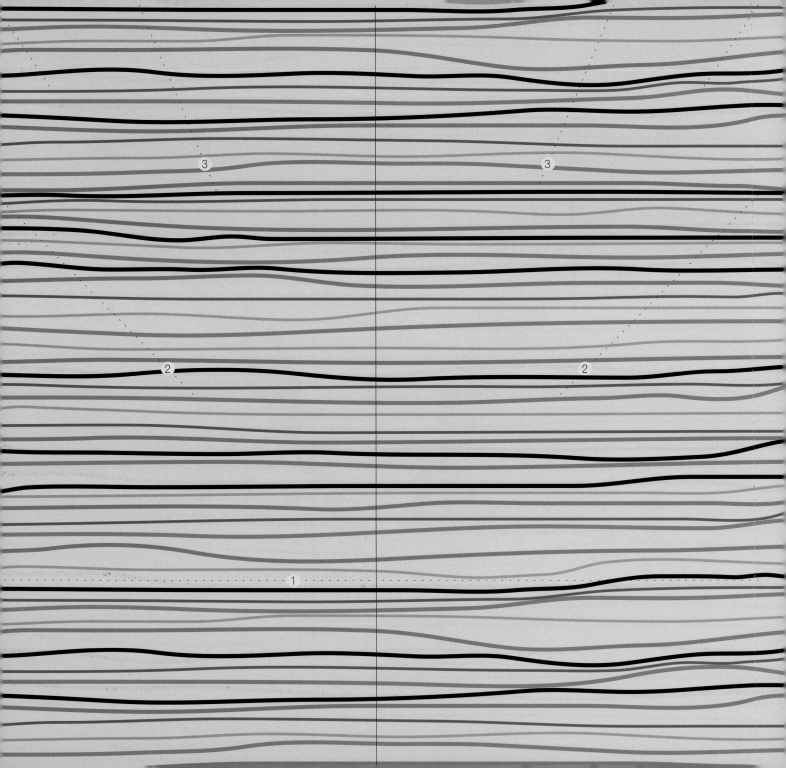

4   ⑤   ⑤   4

WAVE RIDER

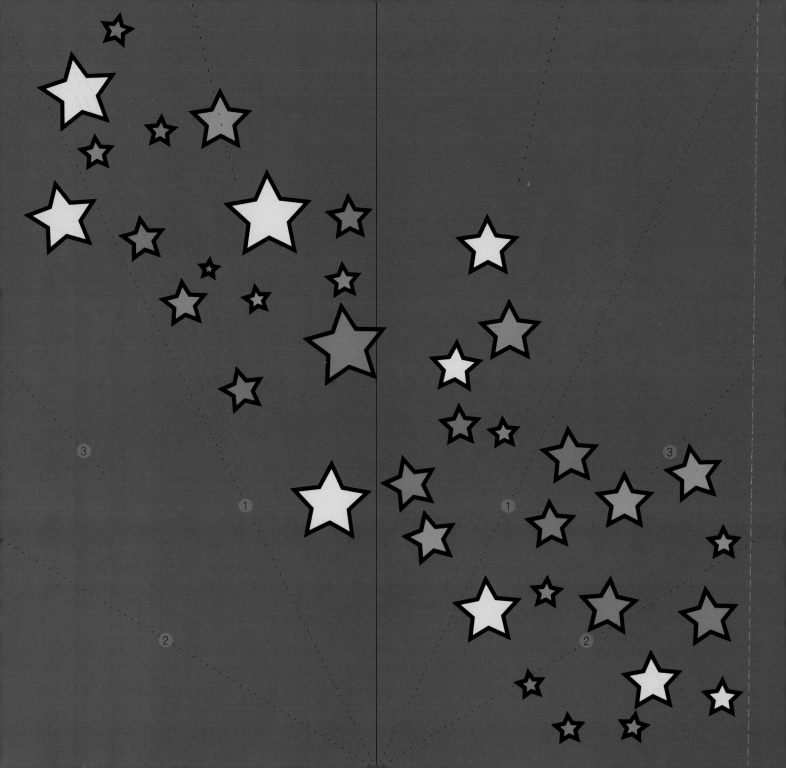

WAVE RIDER

SOARER

CLOUD

CLOUD

CLOUD

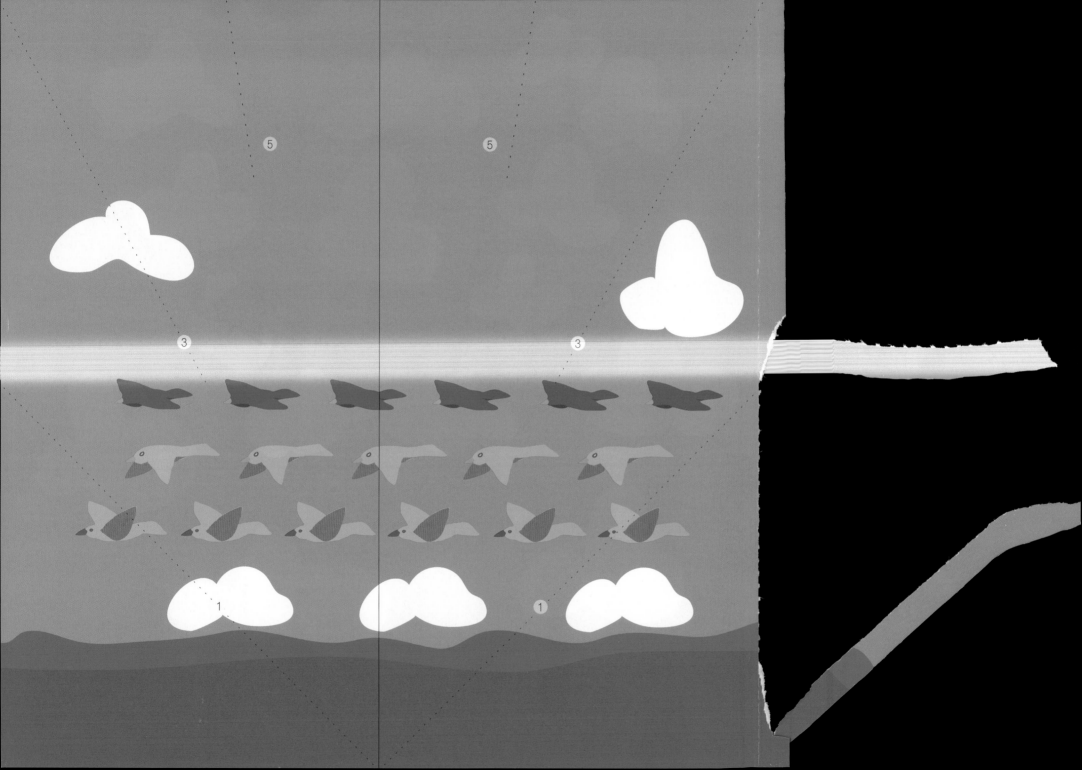

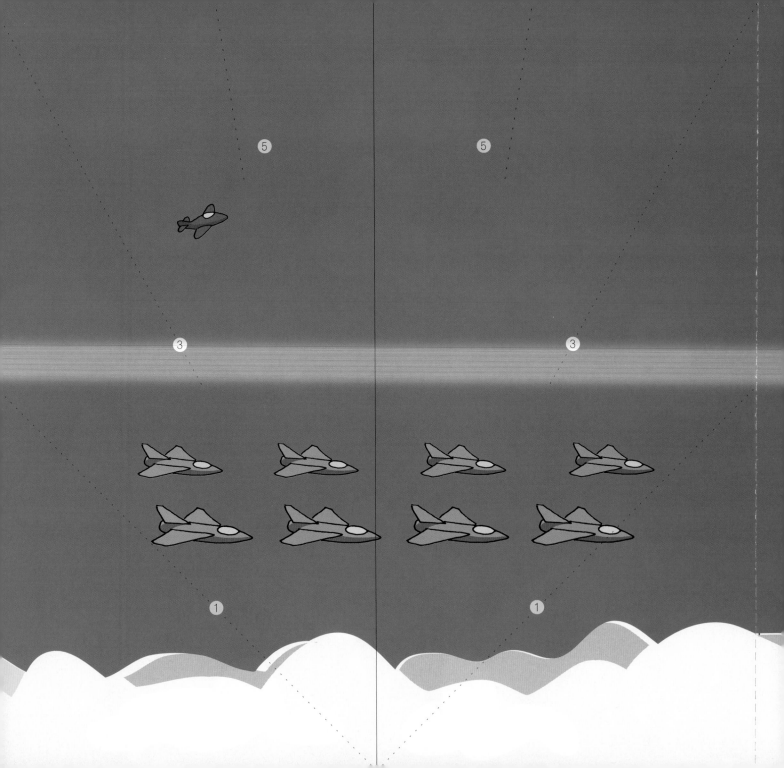

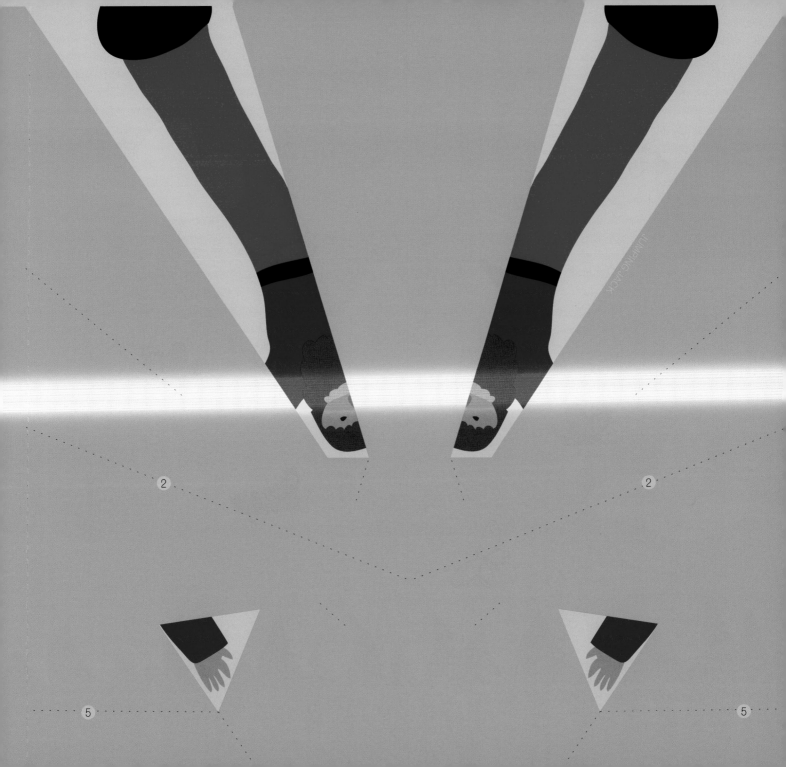

JUMPING JACK

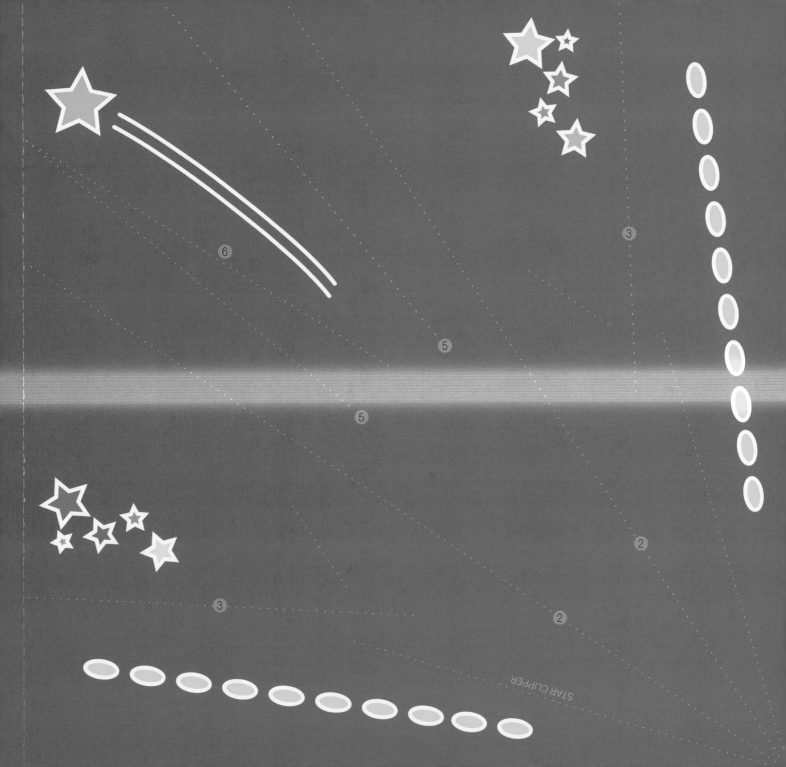

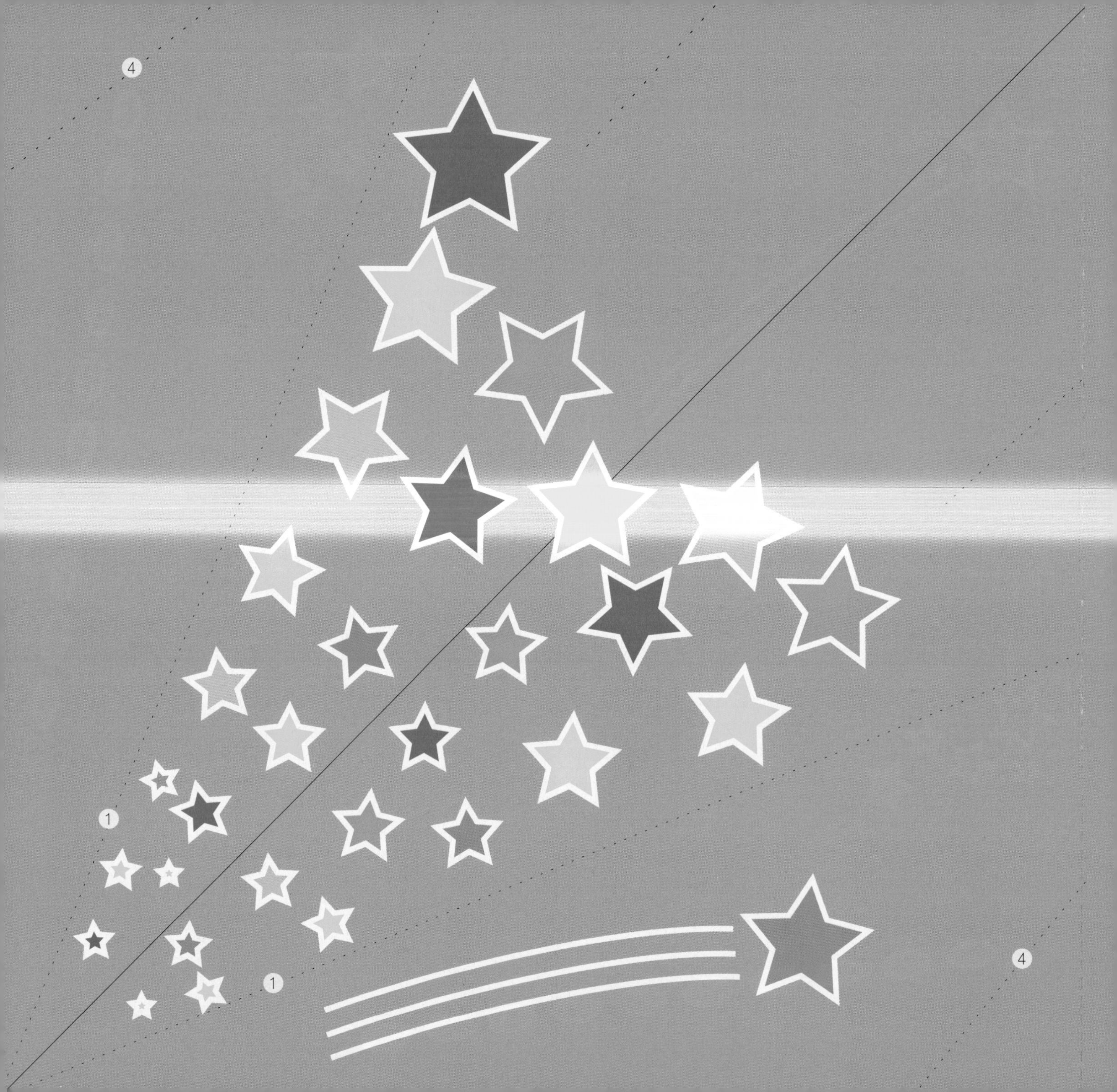
4
1
1
4

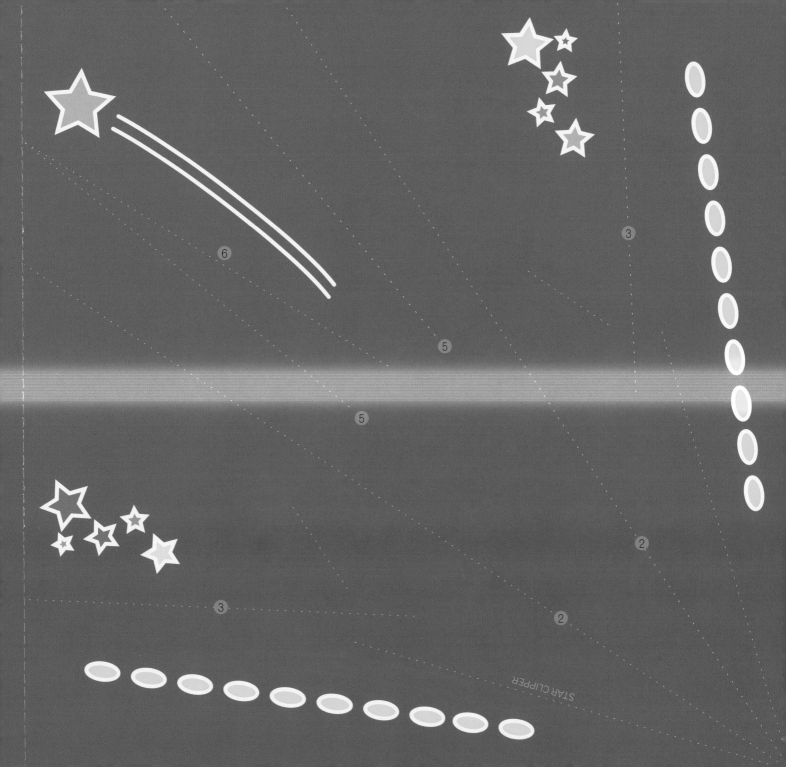

STAR CLIPPER

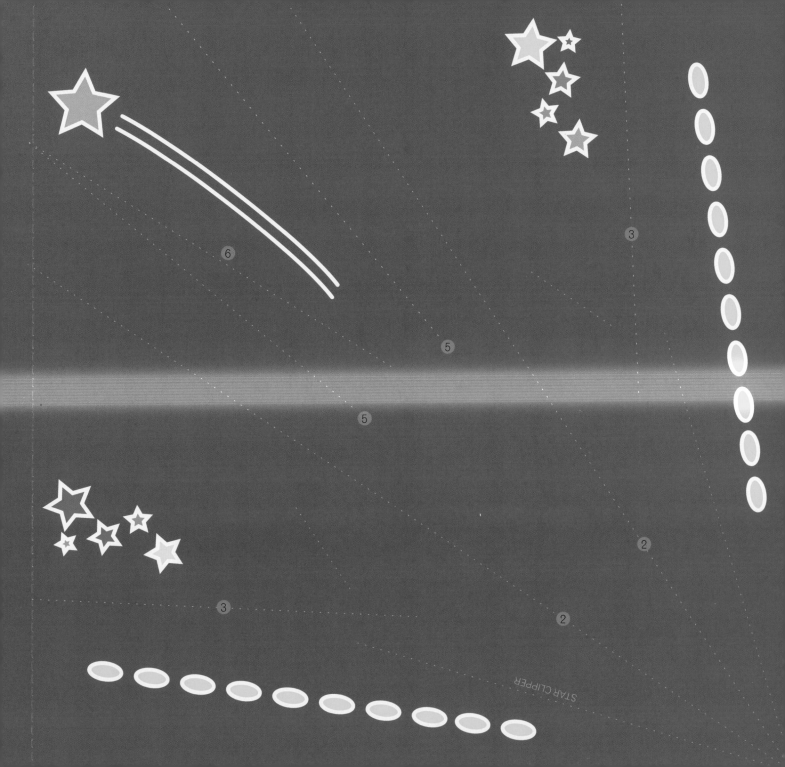

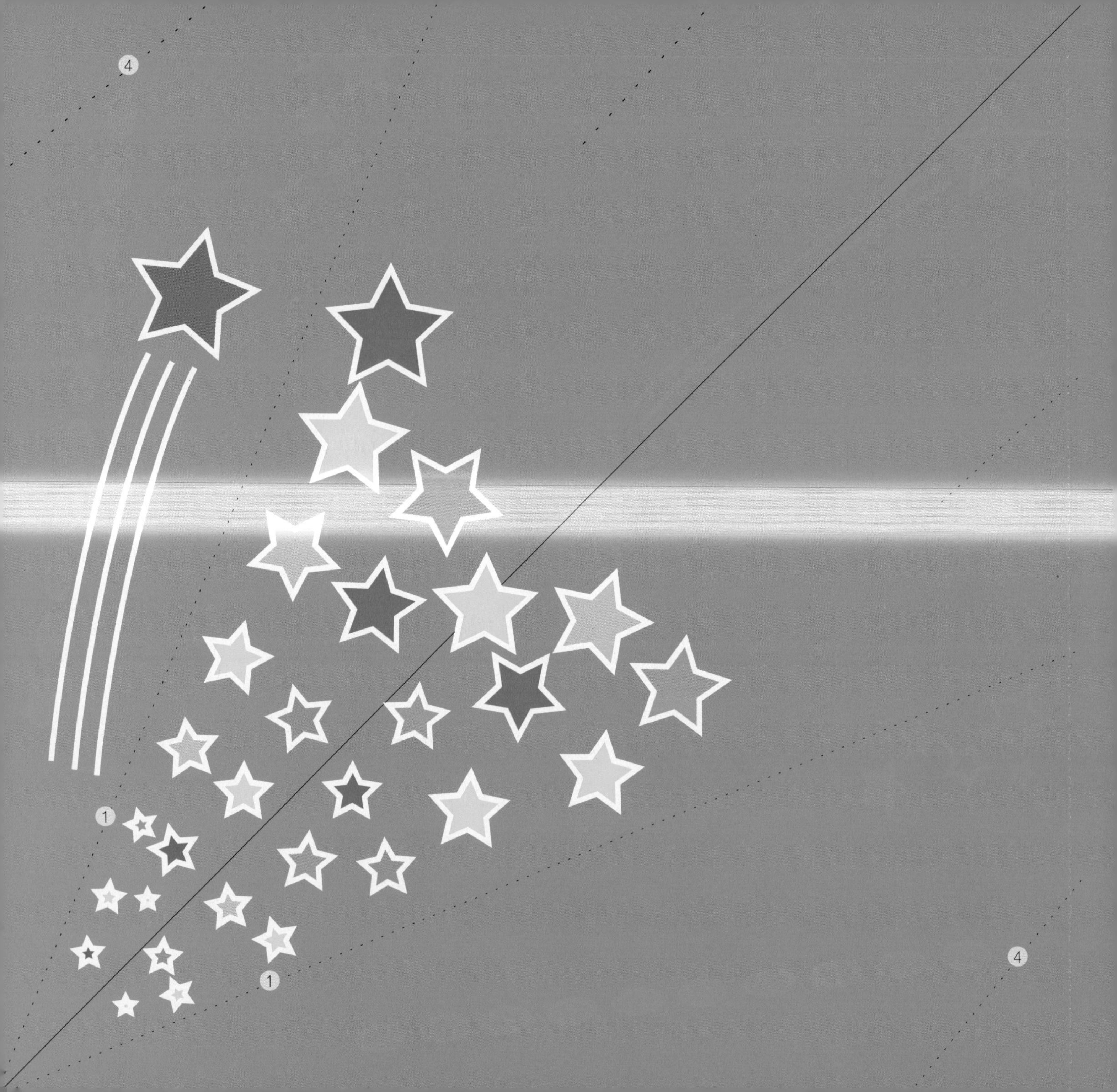
4
1
1
4

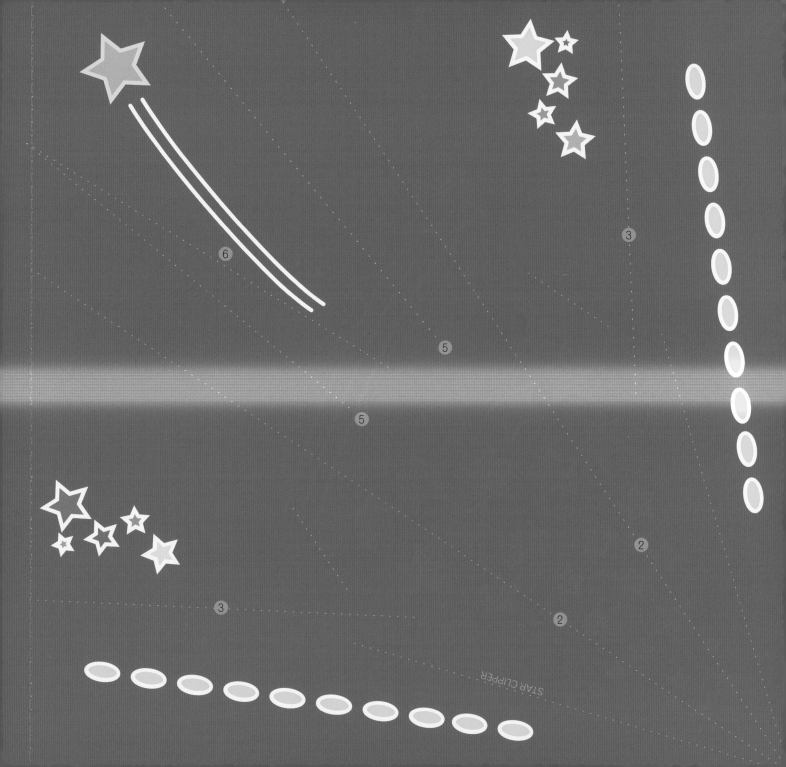

STAR CLIPPER

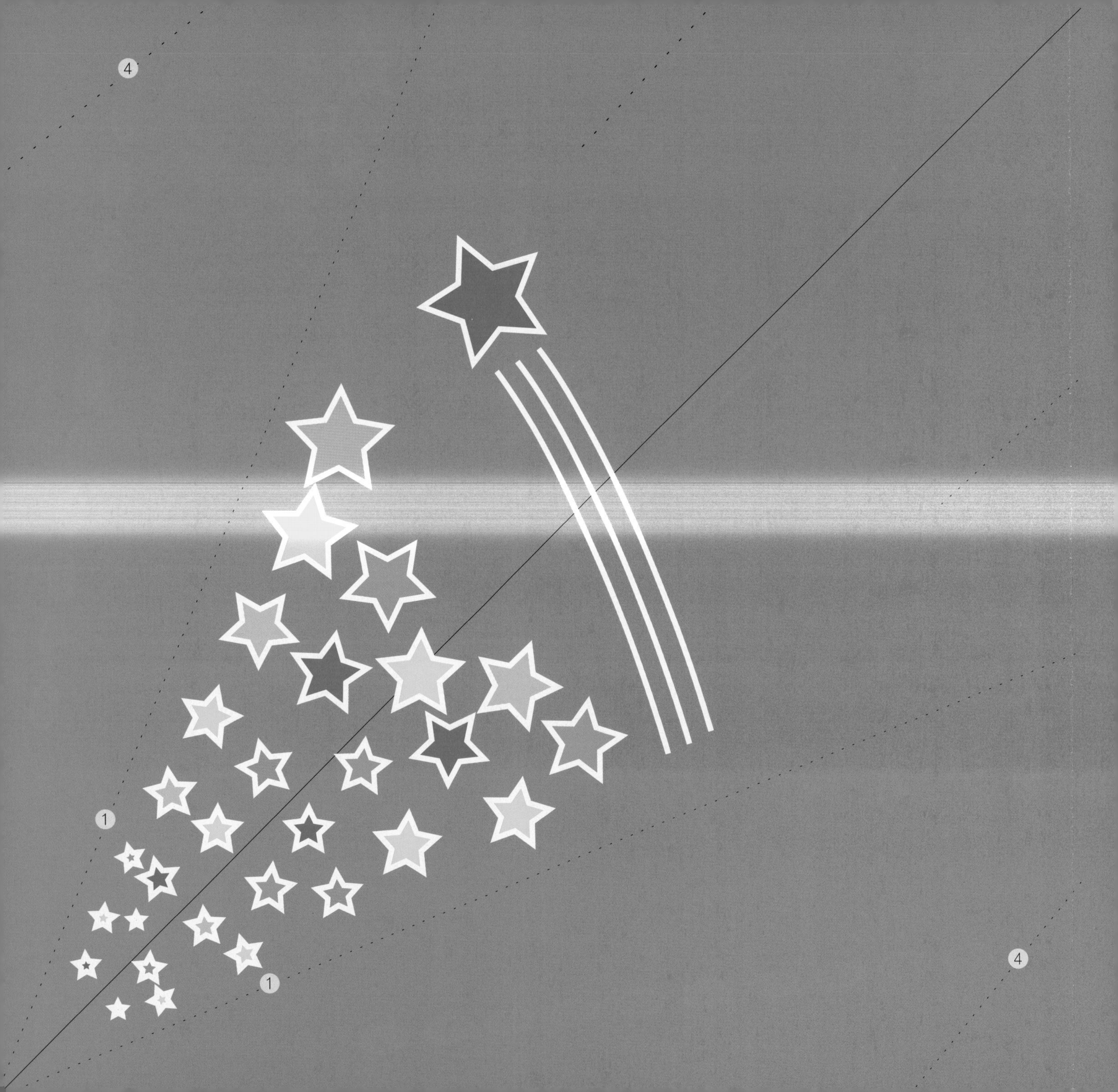
4
1
1
4

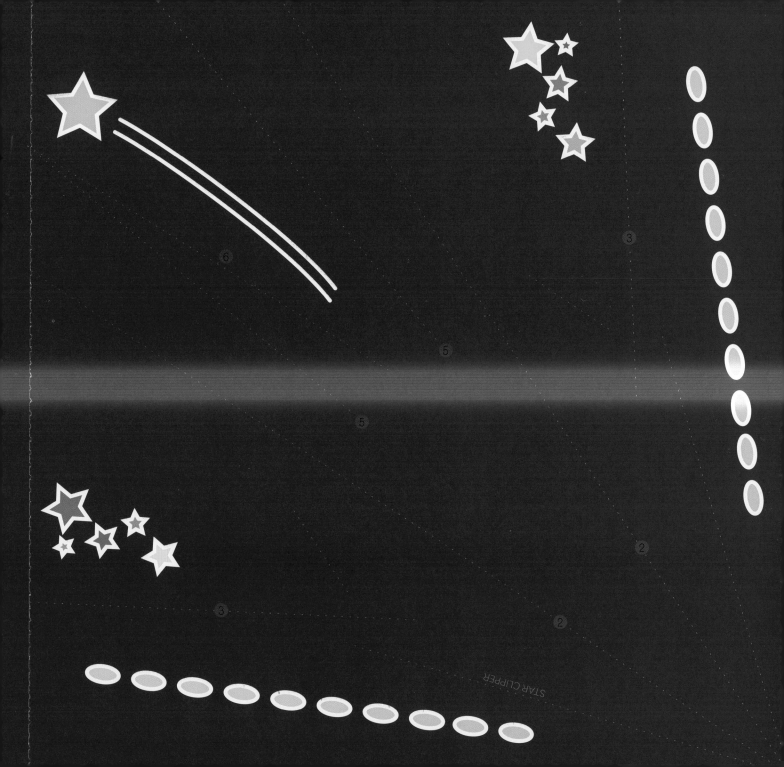

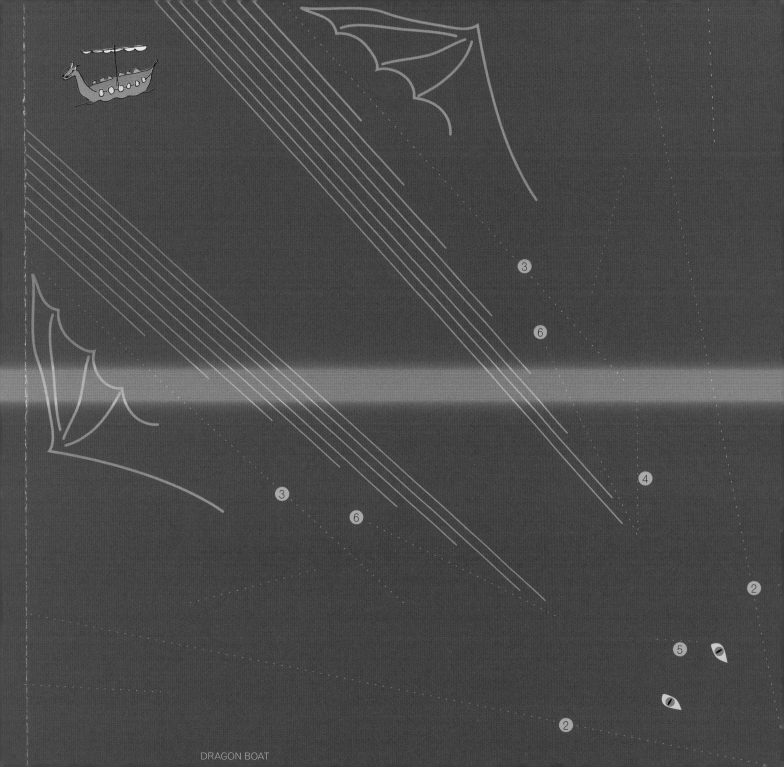

DRAGON BOAT

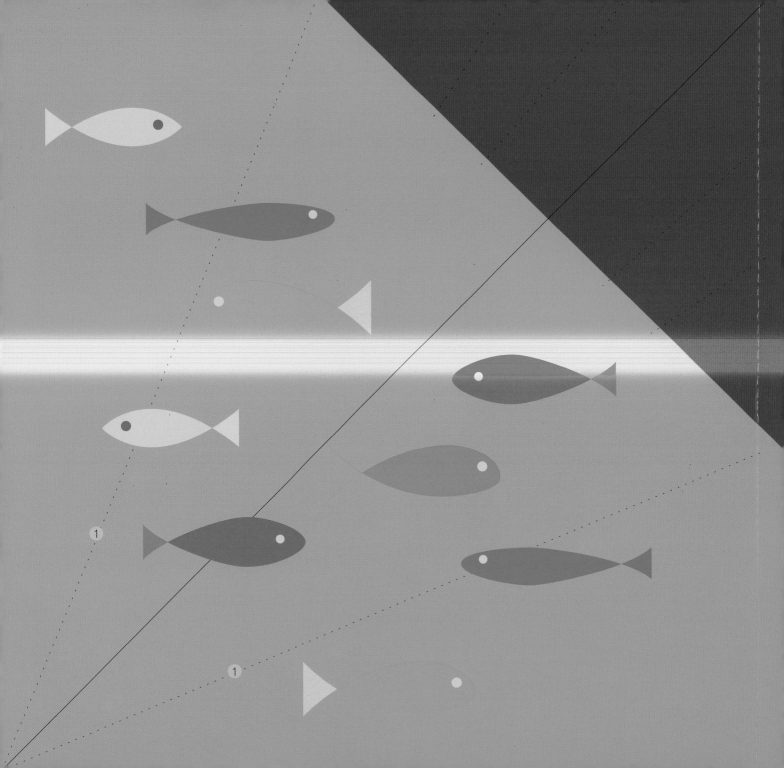

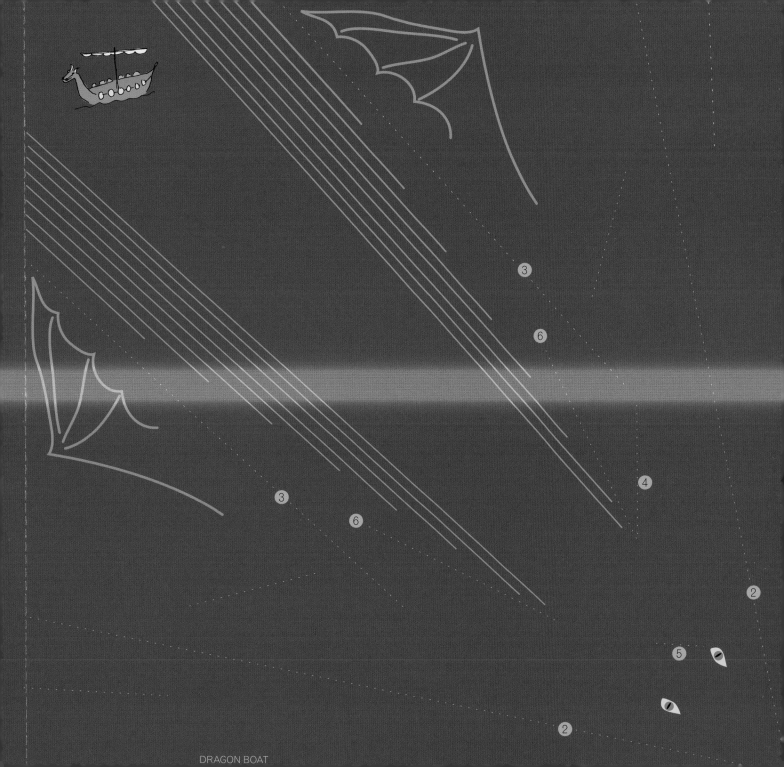

DRAGON BOAT

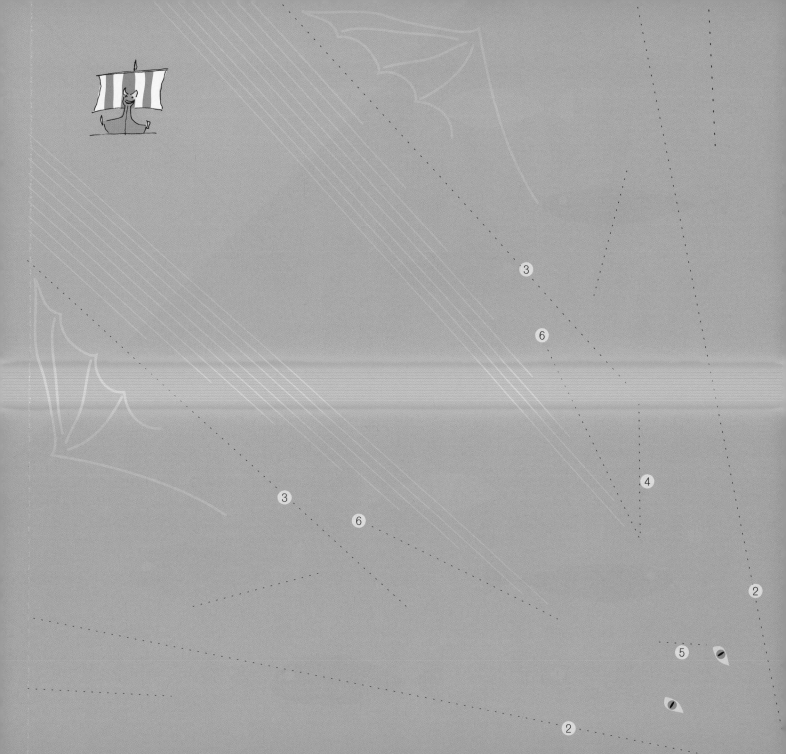

ALPHA JET

ALPHA JET

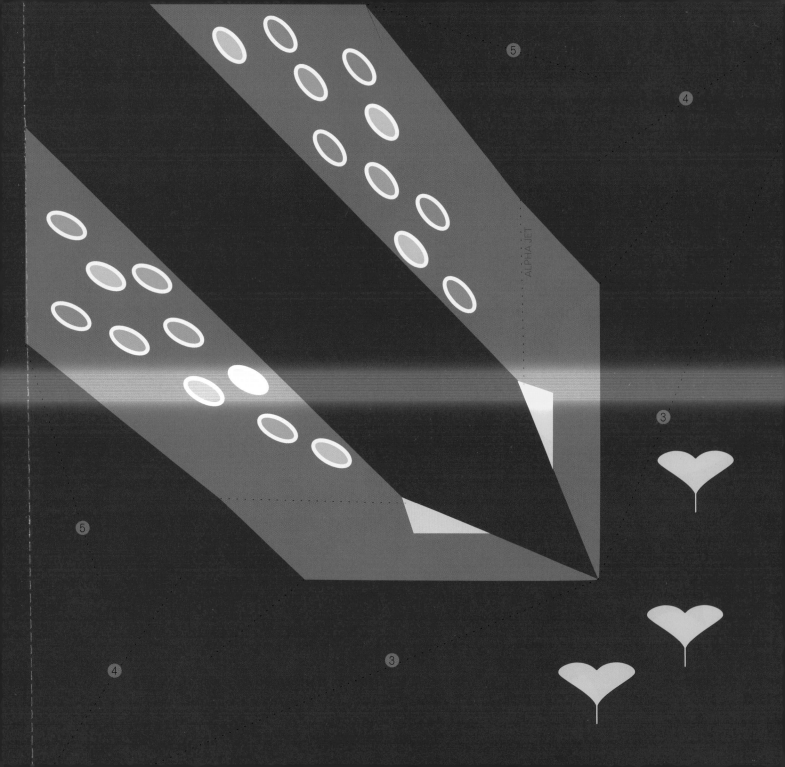

ALPHA JET

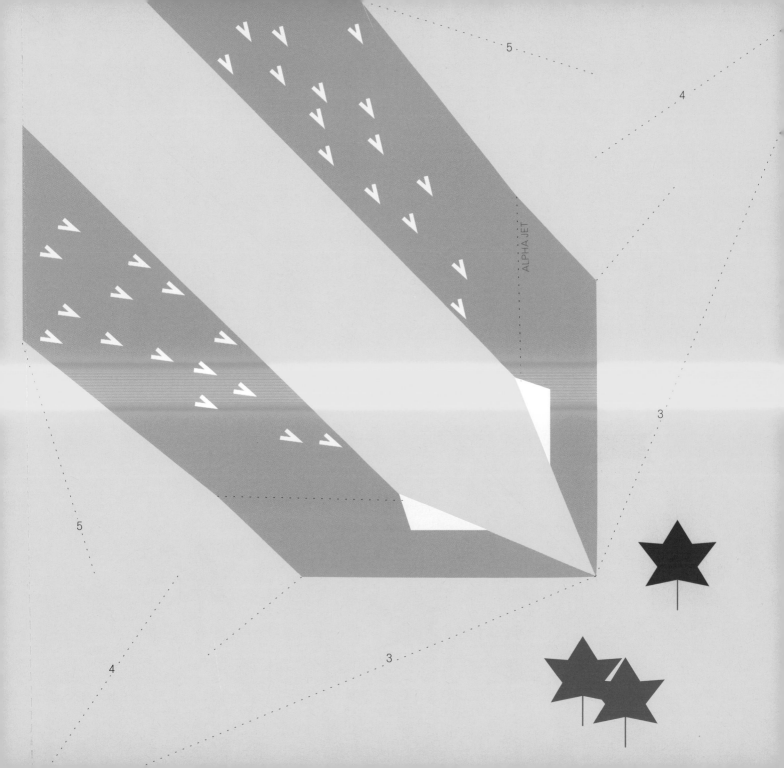

ALPHA JET

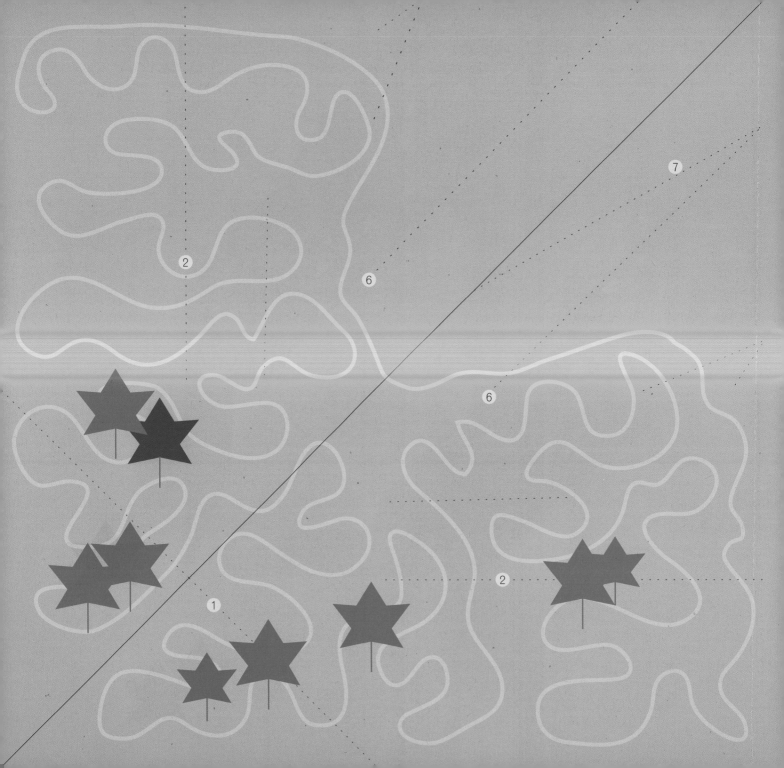

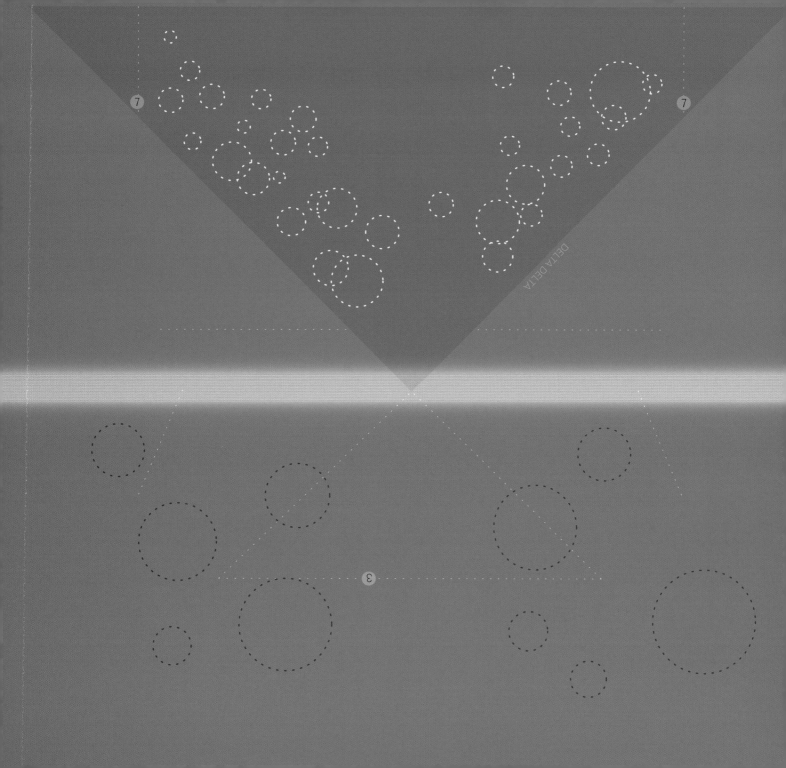

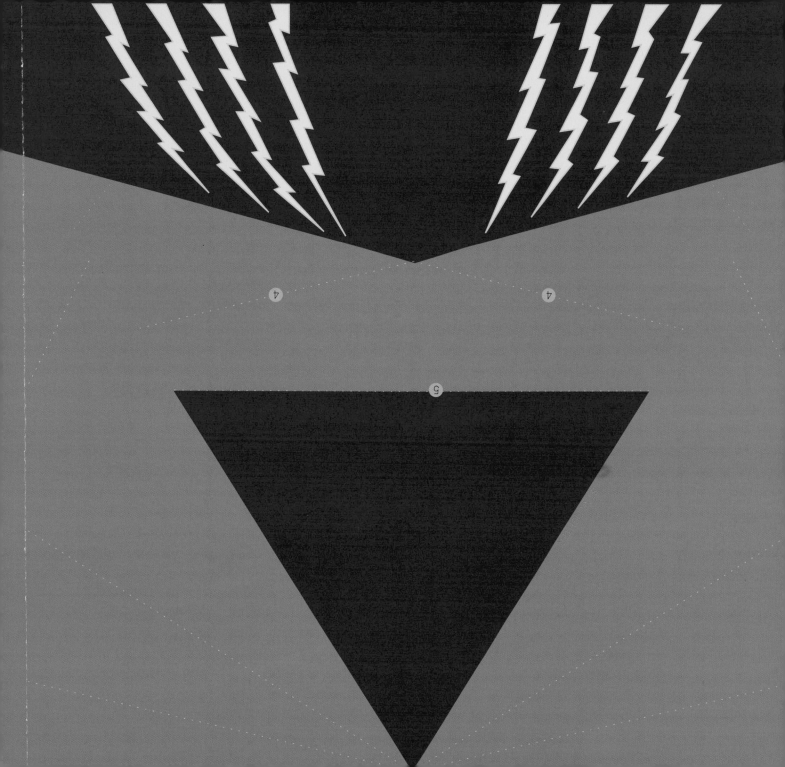

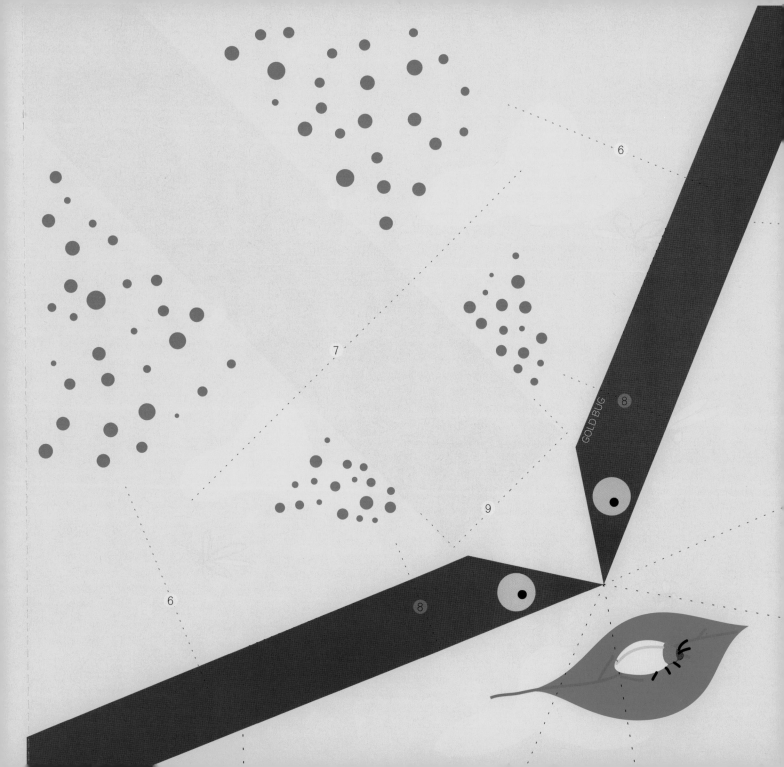

GOLD BUG

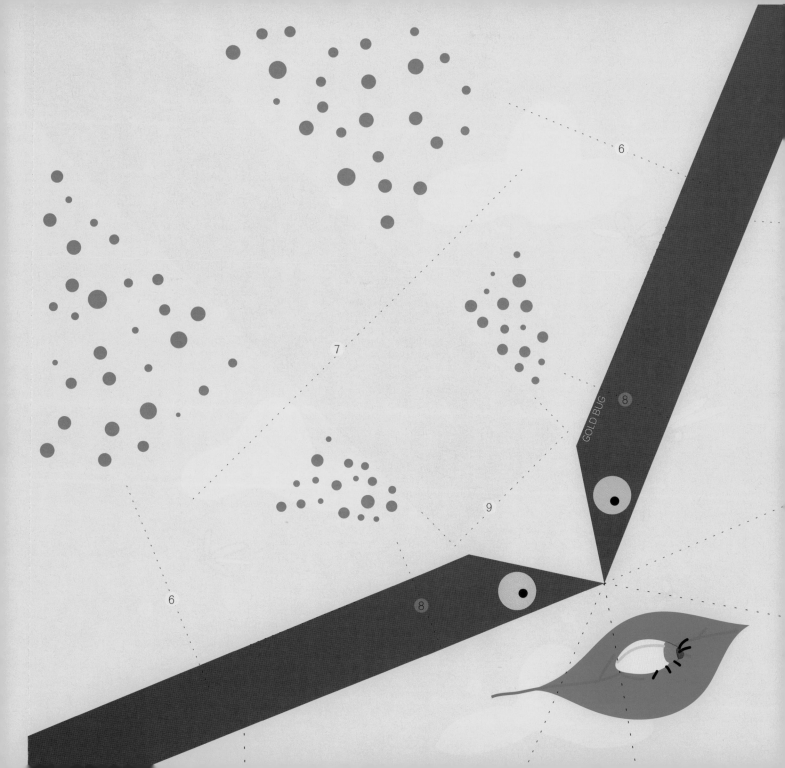

GOLD BUG

6

7

8

9

6

8

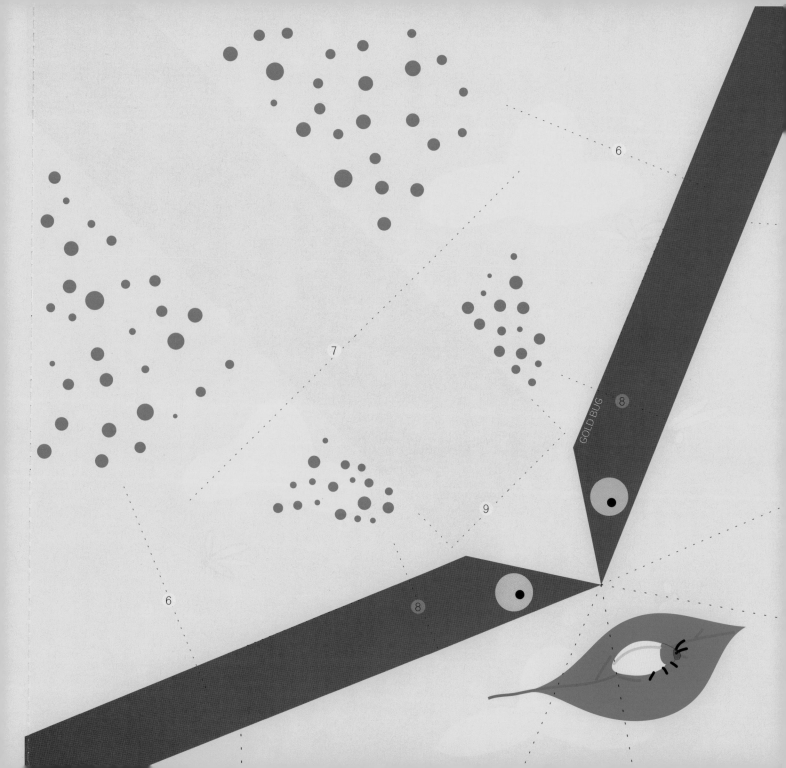

GOLD BUG

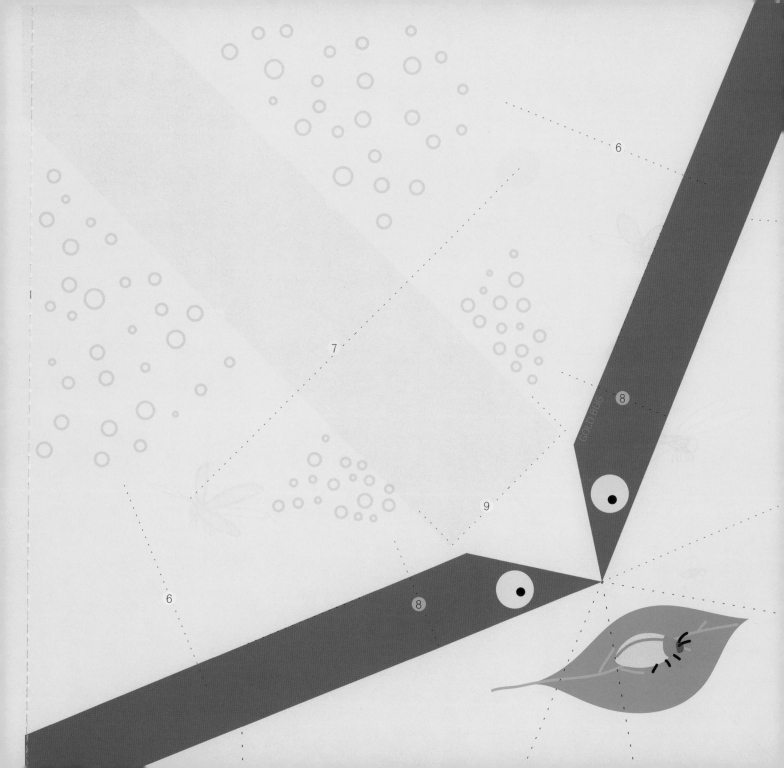

GOLD BUG

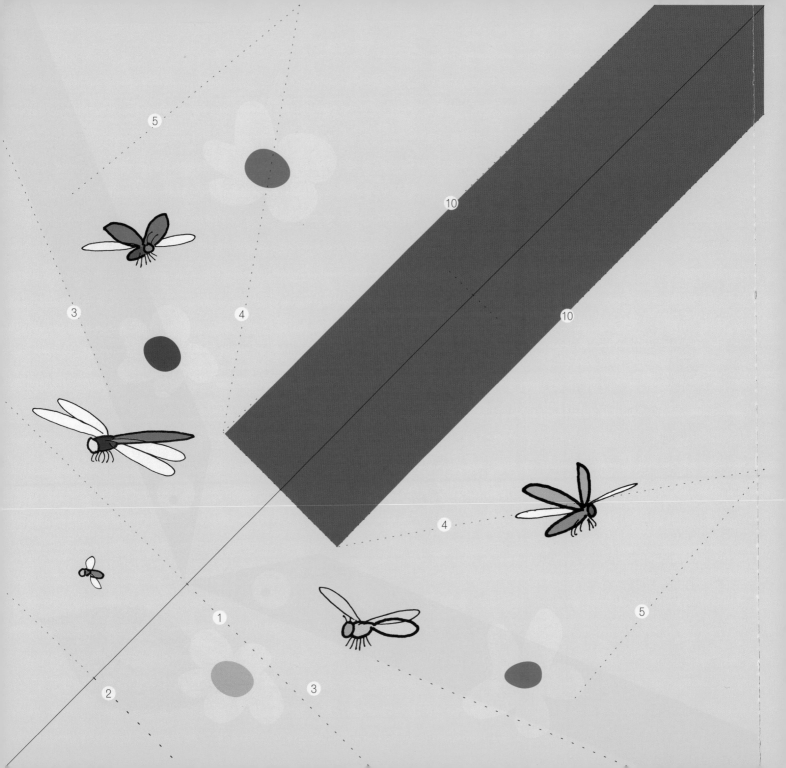

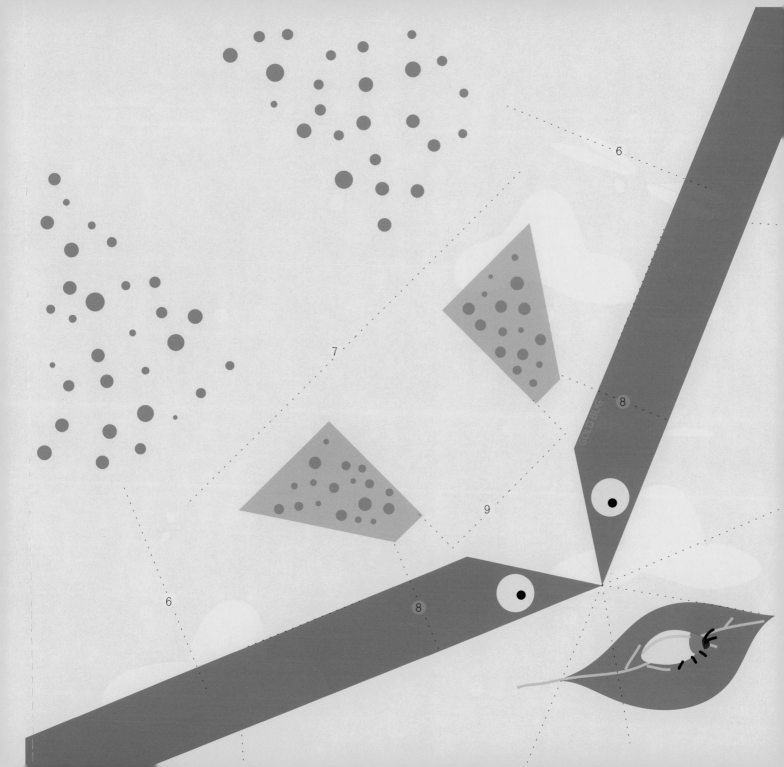

GOLD BUG

おり　み

紙飛機

おり み

紙飛機

おりがみ

おりがみ

おりがみ

おりがみ

おりがみ

おりがみ

おりがみ

おりがみ

おりがみ

おりがみ

おりがみ

おりがみ

おりがみ

おりがみ

おりがみ

⑥

⑤

ヒコーキ

⑥

⑦

⑤

紙飛行機

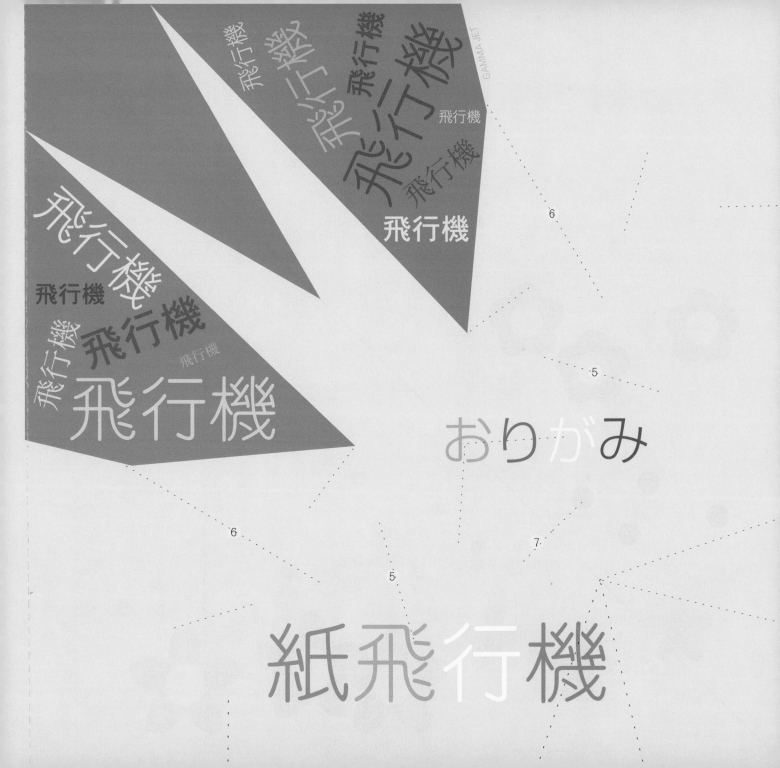

GAMMA JET

飛行機

飛行機

飛行機

飛行機

飛行機

飛行機

飛行機

飛行機

飛行機

飛行機

飛行機

飛行機

飛行機

おりがみ

紙飛行機

6

5

6

5

7

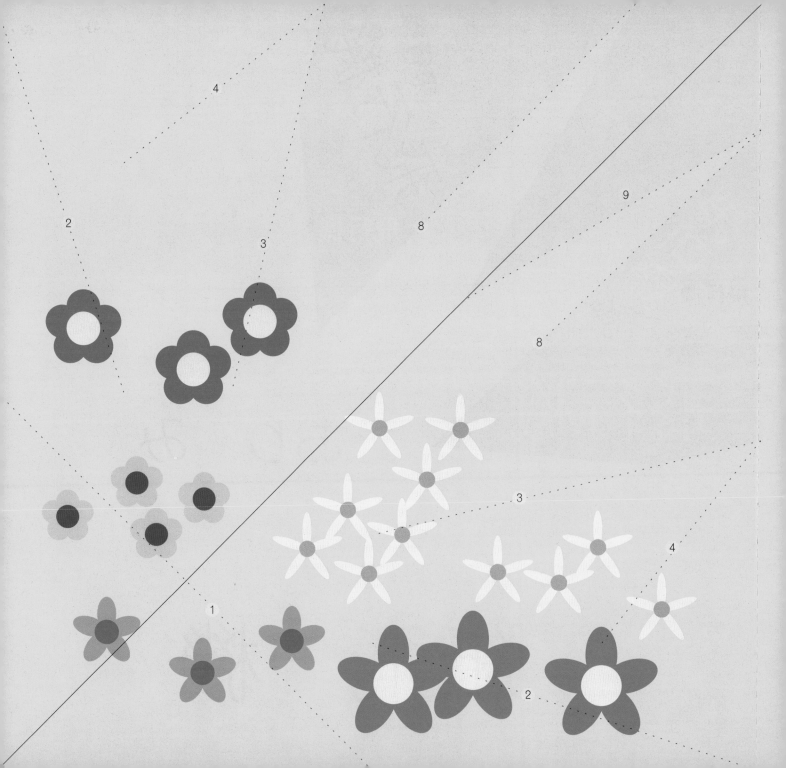

jet *jet* jet

*jet*

GAMMA JET

jet *jet* jet jet jet

⑥

⑤

ジェット

⑥

⑦

⑤

紙飛行機

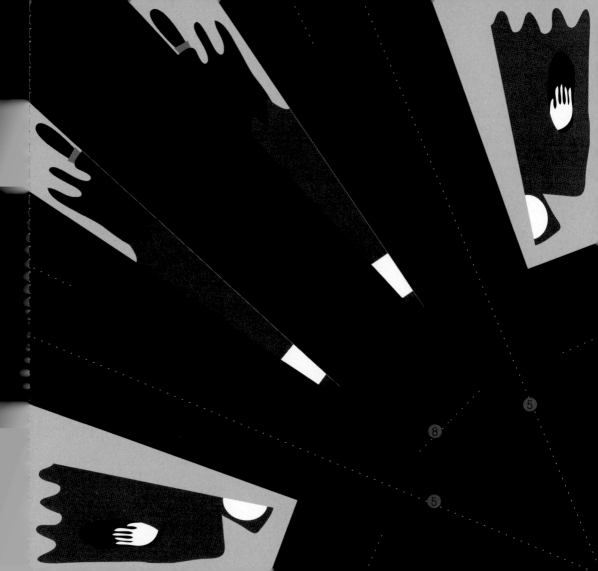

SPECTRE

SPECTRE

⑦

⑤

⑧

⑤

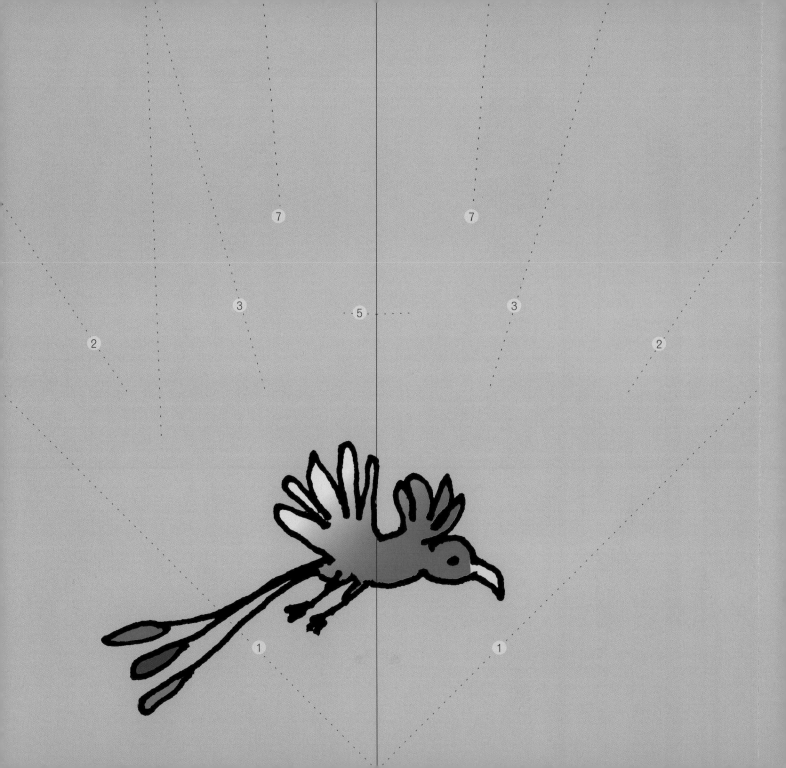

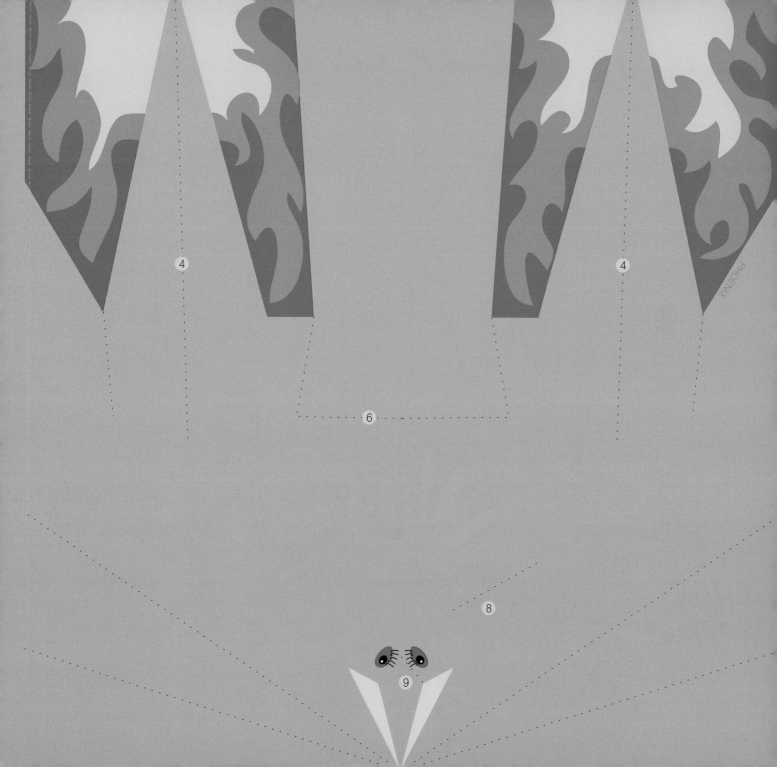

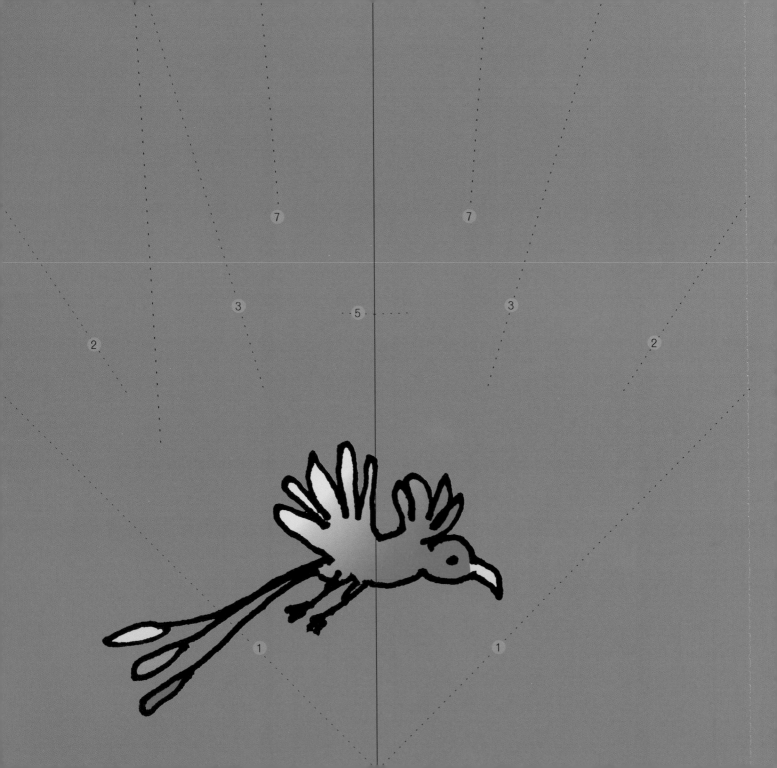

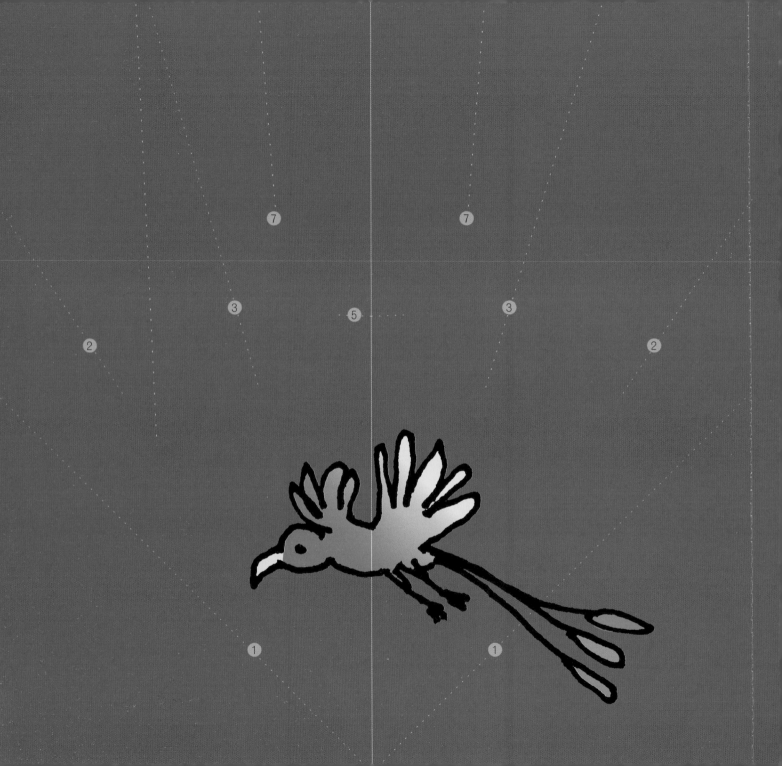

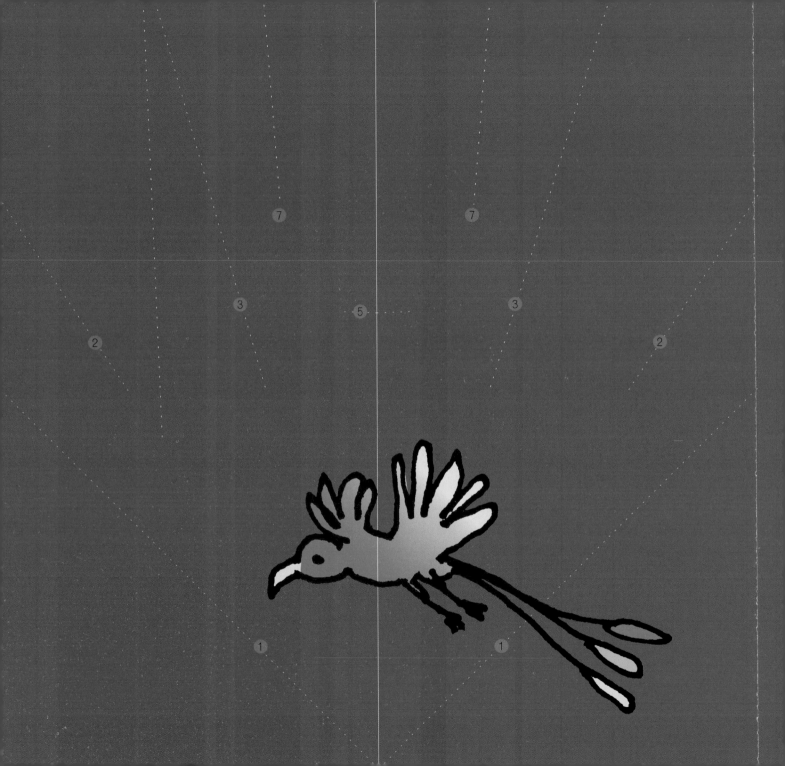

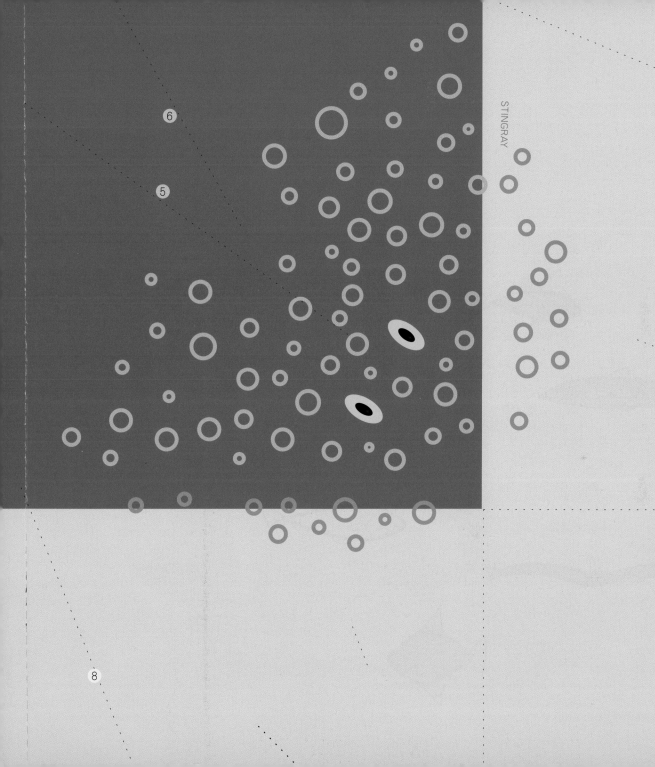

STINGRAY

6

5

8

8

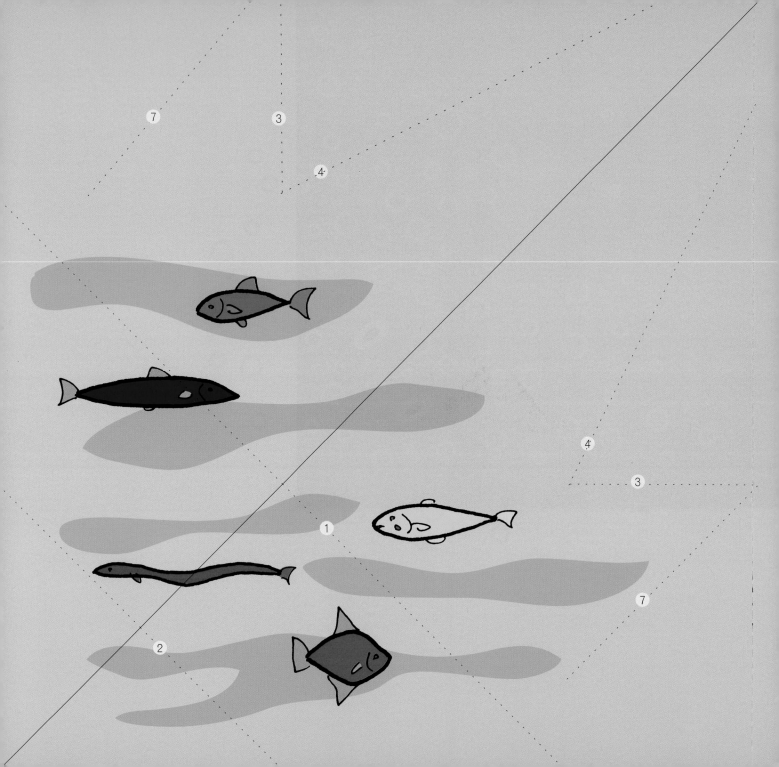

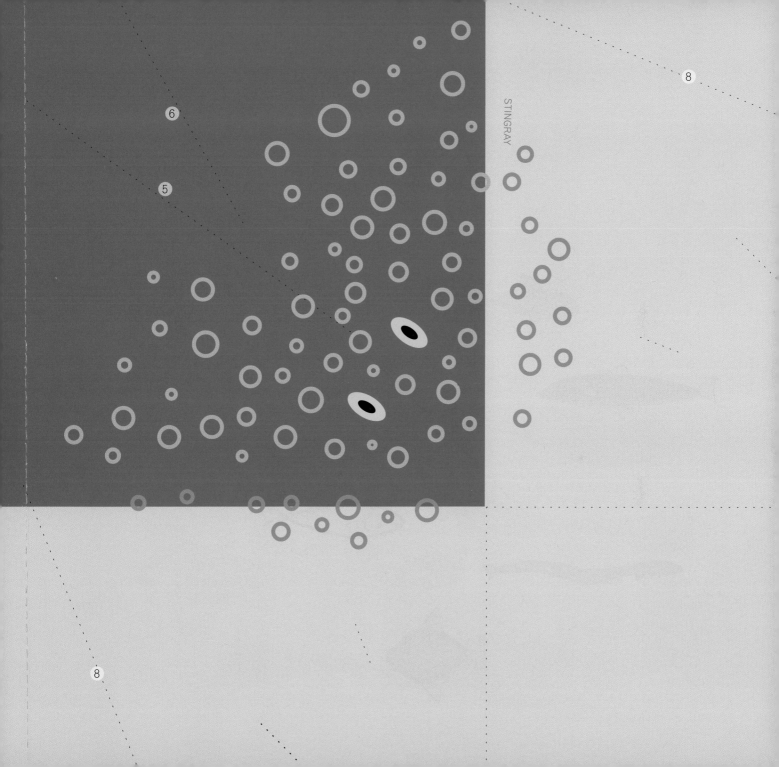

STINGRAY

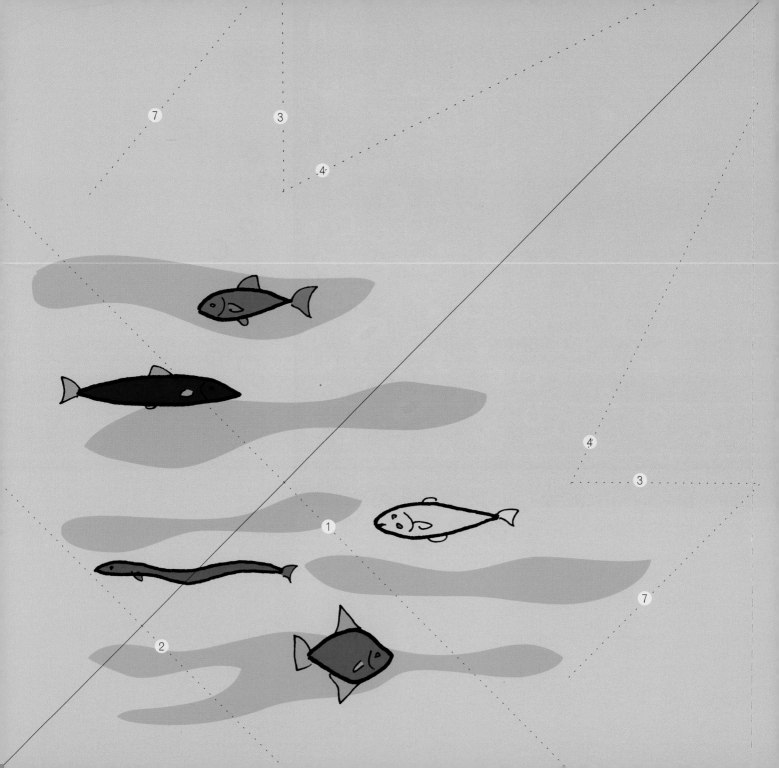

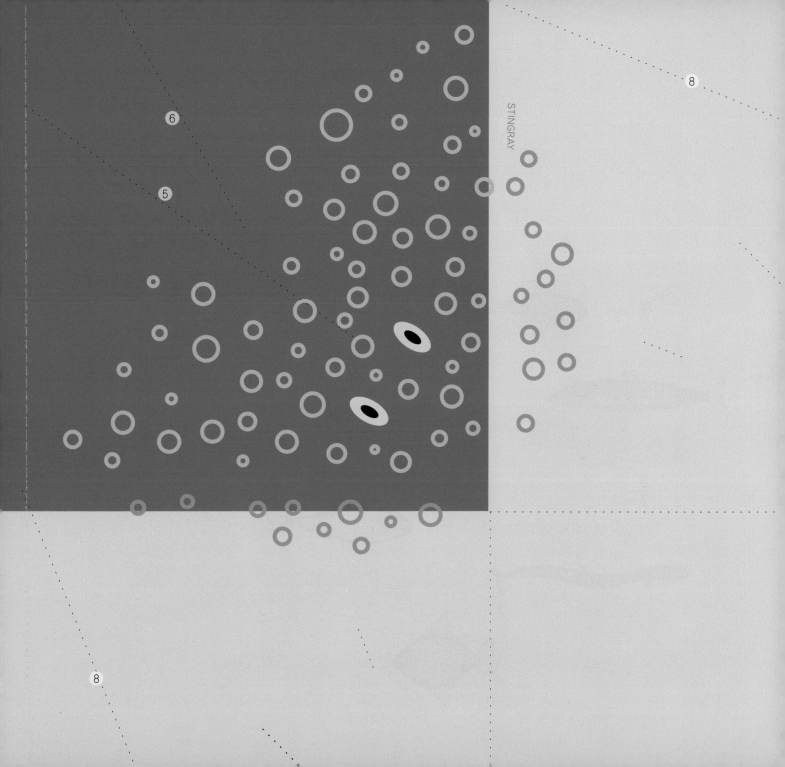

STINGRAY

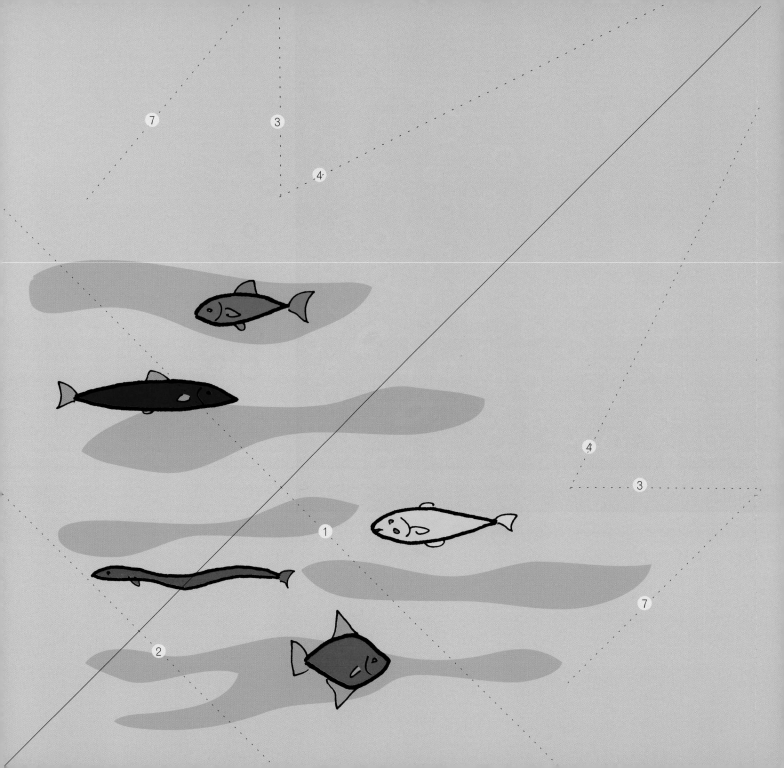

6

5

8

8

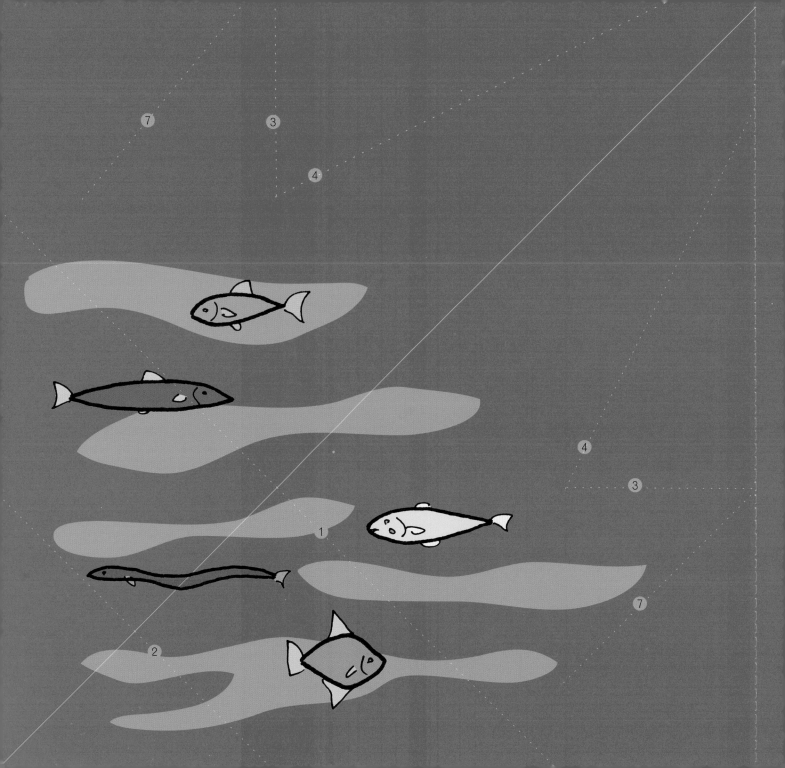

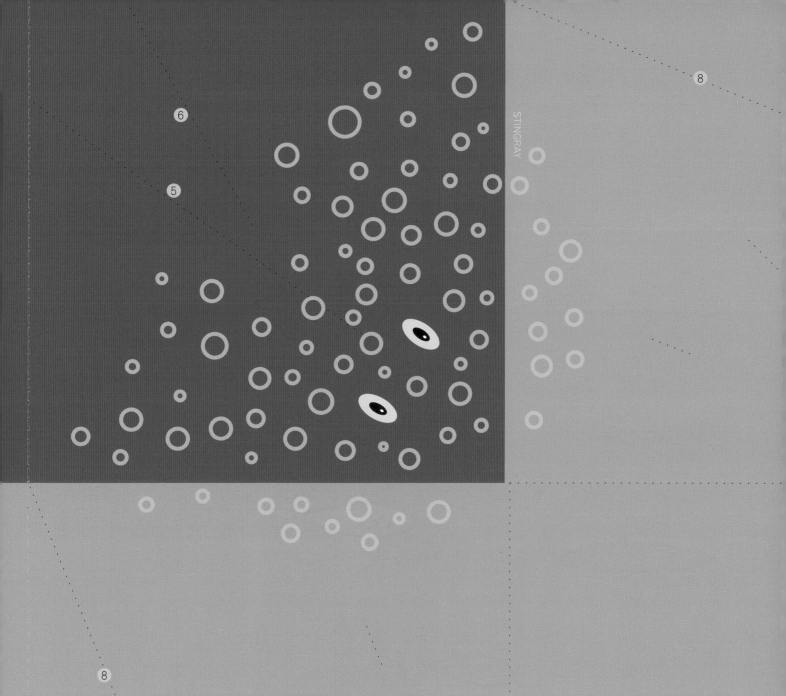

STINGRAY

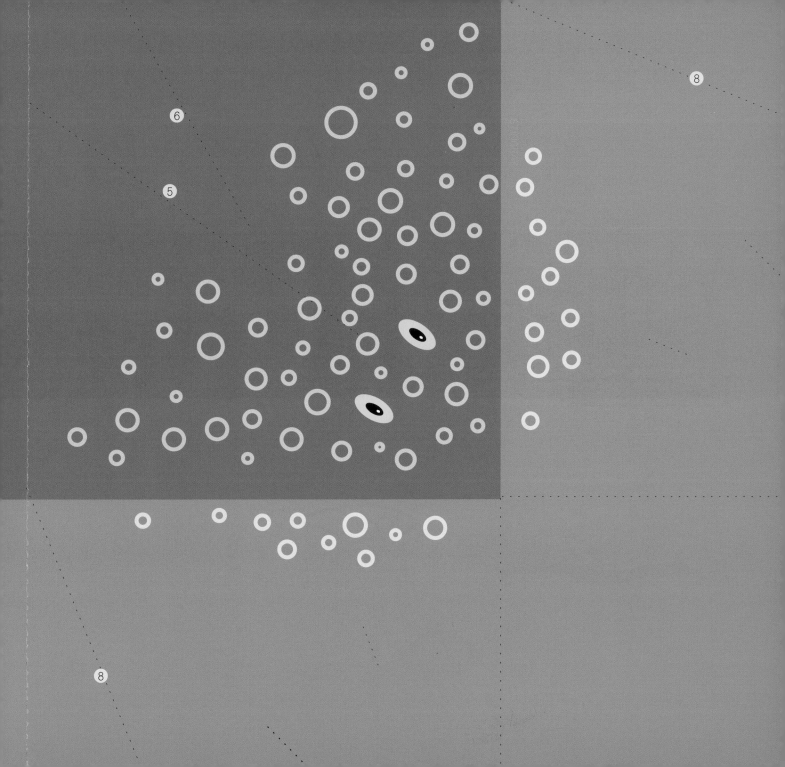

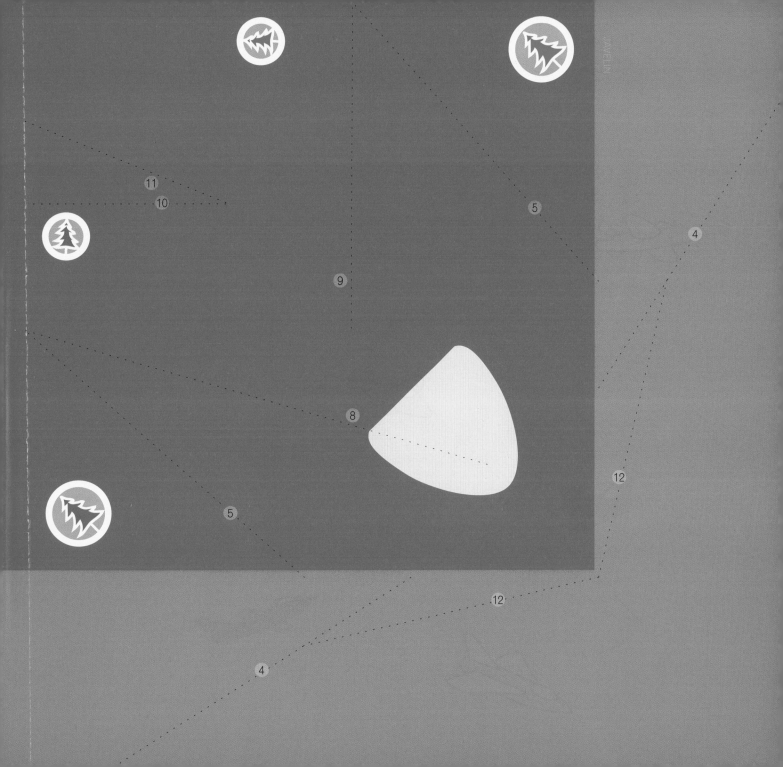

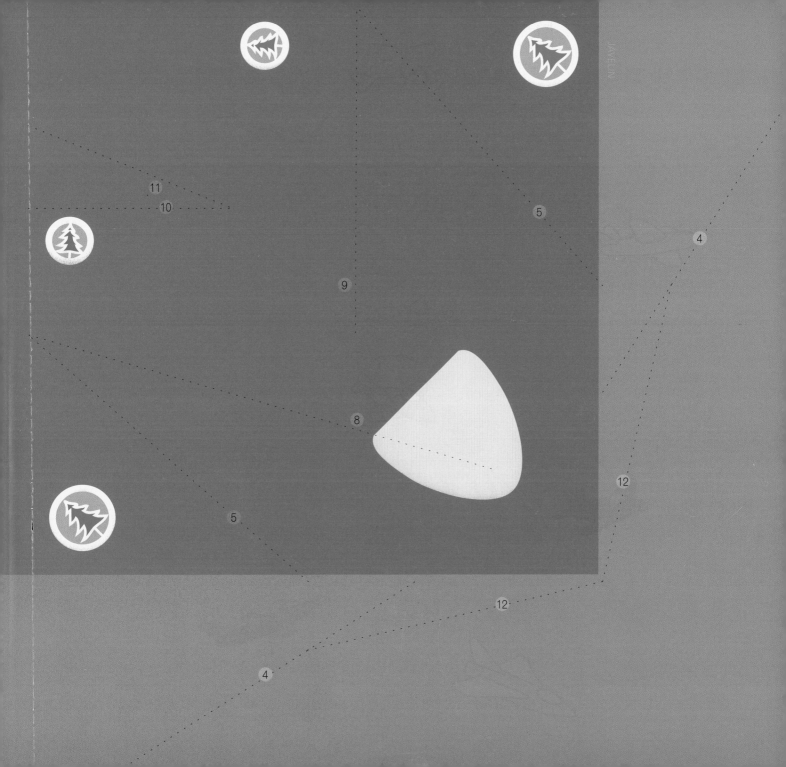

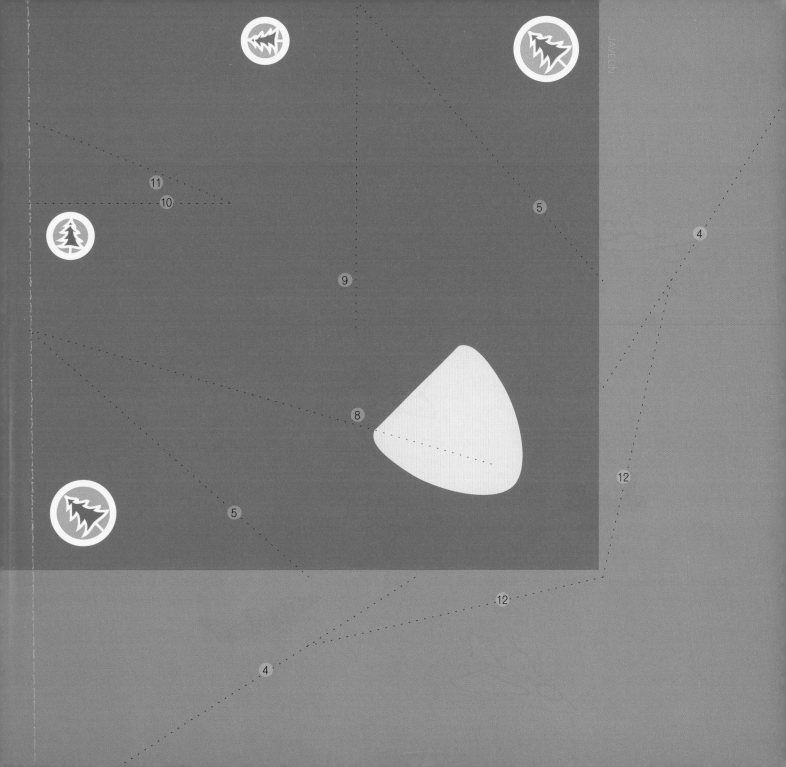

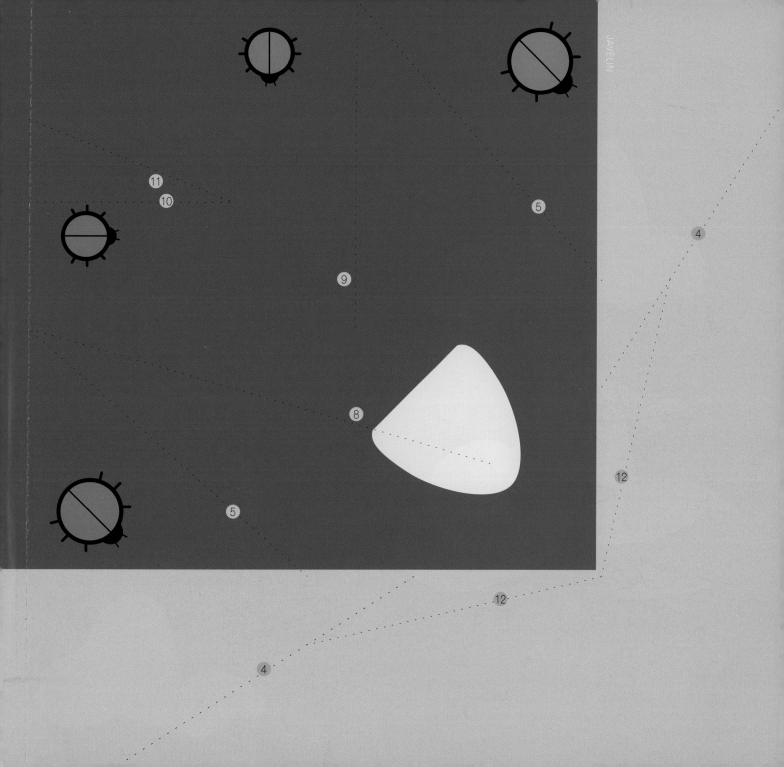

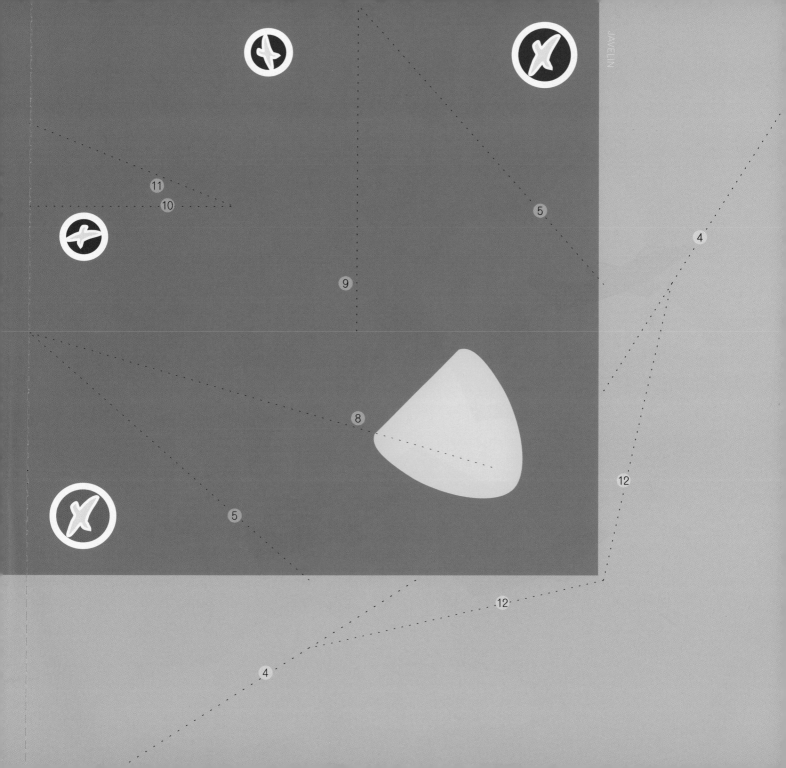

JAVELIN

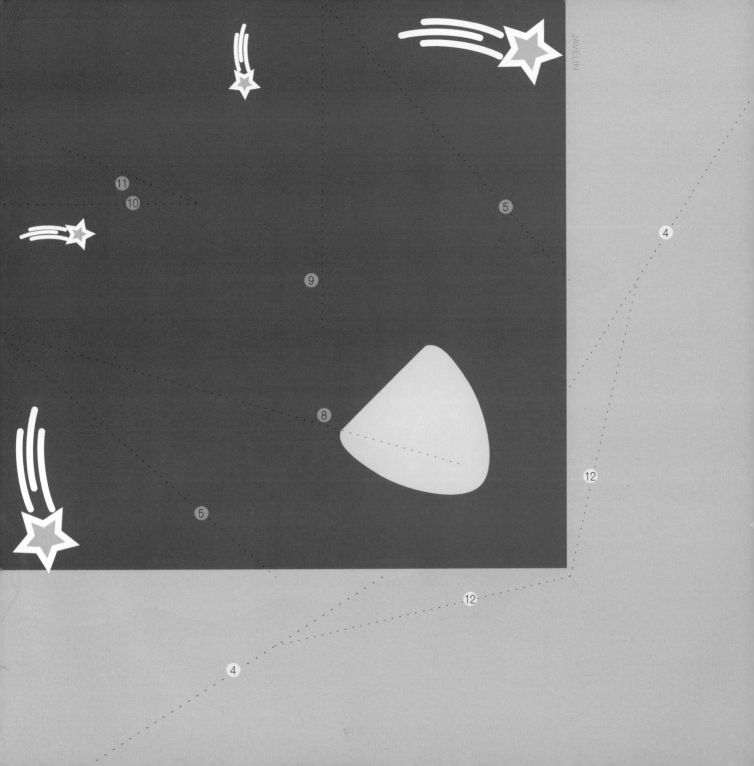